Master the Power of
Self-Hypnosis

C. Roy Hunter, M.S.

Sterling Publishing Co., Inc.
New York

Library of Congress
Cataloging-in-Publications Data
Available

3 5 7 9 10 8 6 4 2

Published 1998 by Sterling Publishing Company, Inc.
387 Park Avenue South, New York, N.Y. 10016
© 1998 by C. Roy Hunter
Distributed in Canada by Sterling Publishing
c/o Canadian Manda Group,
One Atlantic Avenue, Suite 105
Toronto, Ontario, Canada M6K 3E7
Distributed in Great Britain and Europe by Cassell PLC
Wellington House, 125 Strand, London WC2R 0BB, England
Distributed in Australia by Capricorn Link (Australia) Pty Ltd.
P.O. Box 6651, Baulkham Hills, Business Centre, NSW 2153, Australia

Sterling ISBN 0-8069-6351-4

To all who seek to attain their ideal empowerment...

Acknowledgments

My original inspiration for this book was my late mentor and teacher, Charles Tebbetts, who, through both his teaching and personal example, convinced me that the power of the mind is the greatest power in the world and God's greatest gift to the human race.

Additionally, I would like to thank the many hundreds who have personally expressed appreciation to me over the years for teaching the concepts updated and expanded upon in this work. Those praises from my peers not only validate what I've already used and taught, they also honor my late mentor who taught me the art of self-hypnosis. I would also like to express my appreciation to my friends and family, and especially to Jo-Anne for her patience during the many nights she slept alone into the "wee" hours while I finished this book. I'm also grateful to the staff at Sterling for believing enough in my work to publish it.

Finally, I wish to thank *you*, the reader, for choosing this book as your tool to greater empowerment and freedom from old subconscious programming. It is my sincere hope that you find enough valuable information to help you feel an attitude of gratitude for your new awareness. May this book help you attain your *ideal self-empowerment*!

—Roy Hunter
Thanksgiving Season, 1997

Preface
Don E. Gibbons, Ph.D.

As a clinical psychologist, I have conducted considerable research into the benefits of ethical hypnosis and hypnotherapy. That research validates the often-overlooked value of trance as an effective modality to help people attain their full potential.

Roy Hunter, an internationally recognized leader in the field of hypnotherapy, has done much to elevate what many psychologists refer to as "lay hypnotherapy." Roy's work truly deserves to be called professional.

Although he does not have a doctoral degree, I am personally familiar with this author's work. His presentations and training seminars at numerous national hypnosis conventions demonstrate his dedication to hypnosis as a profession; and he has taught college-level hypnosis since 1987.

In 1994 Roy's comprehensive hypnosis text was published by another publisher and received praise from my own profession as well as the hypnotherapy profession. He wrote and maintains the "FAQ" (Frequently Asked Questions) for the worldwide hypnosis newsgroup on the Internet and has written numerous articles as well.

I believe you will find Roy's writing style easy to read, yet filled with valuable insight. Reading his self-hypnosis book will be well worth your time; and you just might learn some techniques that will change your life!

Contents

Part Five
Adding Words of Power

Foreword

Kevin Hogan, Ph.D., D.C.H.

Here is a secret... Empowerment is not a process of the conscious mind. Empowerment is an experience that results from the unconscious mind successfully striving for goals and then experiencing at the conscious level a feeling of control. You can "try" to feel empowered. You can go to a seminar about empowerment and experience, for a short period of time, a feeling of greater control and focus. However, you cannot be empowered at the conscious level if that empowerment is not supported at the unconscious level of the mind!

Your sense of empowerment is about to grow. You are about to embark on a journey with Roy Hunter, one of the world's greatest hypnotherapists. Roy will share with you how to make generative change at the unconscious level of awareness so that you begin to experience greater success, a feeling of control, and the ability to reach and maintain your goals in all aspects of life.

Many books about success and goal achievement fail because they address your mind at the conscious level. Roy Hunter is going to show you how to be in touch with your unconscious mind! What does this mean to you? It means you will finally be able to have the necessary tools for personal growth and empowerment.

This book doesn't stop at this goal, however. You get a few bonuses along the way! You are going to see how other people just like you have experienced success with hypnotic techniques. You are going to be instructed point-for-point on how to work with your unconscious mind.

There will be no guesswork involved. You will learn a brilliant mental confusion technique that will help you ease into sleep at night. Best of all? Roy Hunter is going to answer the most frequently asked questions about hypnosis!

For each person who utilizes the powerful life-changing material in this book, I congratulate you in advance. *Master the Power of Self hypnosis* is the most important and most user-friendly book about self-hypnosis I've read in over a decade.

Your guide is eminently qualified in leading you on a journey through your mind. Along the way, he'll show you how to make a few significant changes at that unconscious level we have been talking about. Your life is about to change. Enjoy the ride. It's going to be exciting!

—Kevin Hogan
Author of *The Psychology of Persuasion:*
How to Persuade Others to Your Way of Thinking

Part One

Introduction
to Self-hypnosis

Chapter 1

The Purpose of This Book

Have you ever tried to change a habit pattern, or become more self-motivated, only to find your subconscious mind resisting?

Motivation programs and habit-control seminars attract multiple millions of dollars annually. People investing in these programs frequently feel frustrated, however, when they find themselves unable to apply what obviously works for others. All of us sometimes find ourselves feeling like slaves to our own subconscious programming. We often get frustrated trying to accomplish seemingly simple goals. We experience inner conflicts between conscious willpower and subconscious desires.

My clients frequently ask me why willpower seems insufficient for overcoming undesired habits. I respond by explaining that acceptance of any new habit pattern requires subconscious cooperation, otherwise subconscious belief in failure undermines your conscious decision to change. A basic law of the mind is at work: *whenever the conscious and subconscious are in conflict, the subconscious invariably wins!* Stated another way, imagination wins out over logic. Professionals call this the *law of conflict*, and this law represents a major reason for subconscious resistance to change.

Subconscious Control

Habits are controlled by the subconscious (often called the right brain) rather than by the conscious mind (often called the left brain). We must effectively motivate the subconscious in order to overcome subconscious resistance and permanently change a habit. All too often we tend to beat up on ourselves when the right brain refuses to buy any of the numerous logical solutions attempted by the left brain.

All of our present habits, mannerisms, and thought patterns are the result of past programming of the subconscious by parents, teachers, peers, coworkers, television—and a variety of other sources. We frequently try to change undesired habits through willpower and/or self-discipline, only to discover logic losing to imagination because of the law of conflict. While many people may convince themselves to take the logical course of action, they still *imagine* themselves following their subconscious desires.

For example, smokers trying to quit still imagine the taste or smell of cigarettes, or dieters imagine how good junk food would taste—only to backslide into old habits. The law of conflict has been proven repeatedly by smokers and dieters, as well as by anyone encountering difficulty trying to attain a goal.

The only lasting solution requires that we reprogram the subconscious; otherwise it will maintain control over our habits. In other words, when we have a right-brain problem, we need a right-brain solution! Hypnosis and/or self-hypnosis can easily and effectively facilitate change at a subconscious level. Increasing numbers of people realize the benefits of trance.

Self-hypnosis helped me so much in changing my own life that I feel compelled to share its secrets with those who are ready to accept and use these valuable secrets. During my years of private practice, I've personally witnessed countless clients change their lives through self-hypnosis. I also believe in the win/win philosophy, so I teach people in both private and group sessions how to sell success to the subconscious—with the personal goal of giving people far more value than they paid for in the first place.

Clients frequently leave my office with new self-help skills. Effective use of these skills will help people feel good about themselves and become more motivated to attain both personal and professional goals. I teach *self-hypnosis for empowerment*, a style of self-hypnosis that empowers the user to enjoy increased control over what goes into the subconscious mind. My goal is to help people attain greater self-empowerment!

Subconscious programming can either propel us into achieving our goals against all odds—or keep us from success in spite of our best efforts. In order to succeed, then, it becomes vitally important for us to learn how to gain and maintain control of our own subconscious programming; otherwise it will control us.

First we must realize that the inner mind responds better to persuasion than to force. At one time or another, virtually all of us have experienced the difficulty of changing a habit pattern. Once the subconscious learns something, it does not like to change; the more we try to force the change, the greater the resistance.

The subconscious is, in a sense, like a rebellious child who resents force. Yet people spend countless megabucks on various self-help books and motivation programs, only to wonder why the subconscious won't buy the wonderful methods that willpower wants to impose.

With the multiple millions of dollars invested annually by various organizations for motivational speakers, it's obvious that people (at least consciously) are *ready for change*. If you are in this group, this book is for you; but first, you must make a commitment to yourself.

Making the Commitment to Change

My own experience illustrates the importance of making the commitment to change the subconscious programming. I discovered this fact the hard way. Allow me to share my journey after success unexpectedly turned into failure...

First, I frustrated myself by reading all the excellent self-help books that worked for others—but somehow failed to work for me. My conscious mind totally accepted the ideas. I even used affirmations too numerous to count—yet justifying failure simply made matters worse. Negative beliefs inhibited me from making a decision to change because I failed to understand the role of the subconscious. At the time I wondered why, and asked successful people for help. They simply told me to change my beliefs.

A typical response one frequently hears from a successful person is, *Whatever you believe, you will achieve*. Of course, successful people frequently go on to expound that if you think positively, you will get positive results. Many people teach that you get exactly what you "program" for in life. Finally I desired in earnest to change my program, but my subconscious resisted. My past proved that I had the ability to succeed, because in 1979 my net worth boasted six digits; yet within two years I was broke and deep in debt!

Certainly, extenuating circumstances played a role in frustrating my best intentions, yet they represented only excuses made up by my mind to justify my rapidly disintegrating motivation. My ego prevented me from admitting that my subconscious had become programmed for failure, as a counselor indicated to me. I felt victimized by other people's lack of integrity, and my fear of failure caused me to imagine more setbacks. Allowing others to influence my own mental programming took its toll; and *negative daydreaming* now defeated my positive thinking. It was time to make a commitment to change my subconscious programming.

That commitment challenged me clear to my soul! This task proved difficult at best—especially with personal and family experiences perceived as failures. (Letting go of the past is easier said than done!) Adding to my frustration was the fact that people who told me what to change could not tell me *how* to change. Worse, some of my friends actually made me feel guilty for being unable to change. I had to make a commitment to change, and to accept responsibility for my own motivation to make the necessary changes. Are you ready to make that same commitment?

Motivation and Responsibility

It's easy to think positively when life fills our cup with positives. We can easily stay motivated while leading active, happy, and healthy lives, but how can one stay motivated and think positively when life seems full of negatives? Do you sometimes mistake the "light at the end of the tunnel" for that of an oncoming train? I've been there and done that! Such a setback proves the importance of staying motivated.

This book shares the secrets to motivating yourself so that you may get up again and keep on going, whether your goals are personal or professional.

Sometimes motivation involves patience. For example, certain career successes may precede their financial benefits by several years—as the decade of the eighties taught me—so we must learn to maintain our self-motivation on a long-term basis. I've learned the hard way that a wall full of plaques and national awards will not pay bills; but a greater income will eventually follow such successes if one stays motivated.

Even if we believe that someone else is responsible for throwing obstacles in our path, let's remember that WE must accept responsibility for the way we respond to others. Do we allow another person to defeat us, or do we *claim our own power of choice* and make the best out of negative experiences? While we may not be able to control others, we most certainly can learn how to control our own actions.

We can allow our minds to be either negatively programmed or positively programmed by our own perceptions and responses to people, places, and things. In short, others most certainly can influence our external environment, but we have total responsibility for our internal responses. We can quit, or we can choose to learn from the experience. Regardless, the subconscious records everything, including our responses and any accompanying emotions—and our subconscious programming will be influenced accordingly.

Remember that you must first make the commitment to change your subconscious programming. Only YOU can make that commitment; then you can use this book to help you along your journey.

What Makes This Book Different?

Countless self-help books tell you *what* to change, but very few teach you *how* to change. Many discuss positive thinking and goal setting, giving you pieces of a jigsaw puzzle, while often leaving you puzzled at how to effectively stay motivated or overcome negative programming. Some books teach visualization, while others emphasize affirmations. For example, many thousands of people attest to the benefits of practicing imagery techniques. Shakti Gawain teaches imagery in her book, *Creative Visualization.* Bernie S. Siegel, M.D., also understands the value and power of visualization, as evidenced in his excellent book, *Love, Medicine & Miracles.* Napoleon Hill gave us a masterpiece by writing *Think and Grow Rich.*

Do you seek affirmations? Go to any metaphysical bookstore and search through the self-help books. Affirmations abound in many of these books, along with encouragement to read applicable affirmations many times daily. Why do affirmations often fail?

Additionally, during the second half of the 20th century the number of self-help books has exploded, including hundreds of self-hypnosis books written by authors of varying credentials. You can find many to choose from in almost any bookstore. I don't discount any of the techniques mentioned above. In fact, this book discusses not only visualization, affirmations, and self-hypnosis, as well as goals—and more—but it also teaches you how to reprogram your own subconscious mind!

This is a *self-hypnosis handbook.* I explain self-hypnosis in simple language, and then step you through several creative self-hypnosis exercises, beginning with basic relaxation. I often refer to a mental exercise as an *empowerment exercise.* For the curious, I have even included one chapter on trance history.

Next, I reveal several simple but effective methods of creating your own trance. The book explains how the subconscious mind is programmed and follows with some exercises for managing stress and going to sleep at night.

I explore various traps caused by negative thinking and how to escape from them so that you may clear the obstacles from your journey through life. I also present a meditation into past successes in order to help build confidence and establish a trigger for peak performance. Additionally, the reader will learn how to establish priorities for important goals through another creative self-hypnosis exercise, as well as how to sell success to the subconscious through creative daydreaming. This chapter also provides numerous self-hypnosis techniques for a variety of goals and is followed by two important chapters concerning the power of words and affirmations.

After mastering the self-hypnosis exercises, you may combine creative daydreaming with the proper use of affirmations for a very effective form of creative self-hypnosis for self-empowerment and motivation. I call this final mental exercise *HypnoCise* (the original title for my first book about self-hypnosis).

Although I teach many concepts that others have practiced for decades, I blend them with important new information and valuable insights gained from fifteen years of professional experience with hypnotherapy. *This book shows you how to put those pieces together in a way that really works!* I have a unique way of combining all the pieces to increase the power of self-hypnosis.

You will learn how to motivate your subconscious to help you achieve your goals and how to replace negative programming with positive programming. You will then be responsible for how you use what you learn. Used properly, self-hypnosis will enable you to put what you choose into your own subconscious mind. Self-hypnosis will enable you to become more motivated to take control of your own life, so that you may enjoy and master the power of self-hypnosis!

How to Use This Book

You may have already noticed from the table of contents that I divided this book into five parts in order to facilitate mastering the material presented. You may skim through my entire book in one sitting for an overview if you wish; but you will gain greater benefit by spending at least five self-help sessions at separate times to digest and use the material presented. Practice any appropriate exercises in each part at least once before moving on to the next part.

In these pages you will find numerous references to smokers and people wishing to lose weight. I include these examples to help illustrate important concepts. Let me state for the record that I have no brief to try to get anyone to diet or to quit smoking, except when that person *chooses* to do so. Others might wish to convince you to overcome a habit; but you can say either yes or no. In order for this book to serve you, you must be the one seeking change because your journey through life belongs to you!

Numerous mental exercises enable you to discover the power of imagination. Rather than simply reading about them, DO them! Also, take time to master those self-hypnosis exercises that pertain to your goals. These exercises can help you gain skills that will last a lifetime and may benefit many areas of your life. If you don't follow this advice, this book could become one more "dust collector" on your book-shelf.

Other books tell you *what* to change; this one teaches you HOW to get your subconscious to buy the changes you choose. You may use *Master the Power of Self-hypnosis* to help you attain your goals along your journey through life. You could also say that my purpose in writing this book is to teach you how to *win with both sides of the brain!*

Chapter 2

What Is Hypnosis?

Have you ever cried real tears during a powerful movie? Your conscious mind maintained awareness of your sitting in a theater watching actors and actresses, but your subconscious accepted the movie stars as real characters. Believe it or not, you probably entered the state of hypnosis! Since the subconscious doesn't know the difference between fact and fantasy, we respond emotionally to what happens on screen. People jump or scream during a scary movie—or get excited during a juicy romance scene—yet the conscious mind knows it's only a movie. I can still remember the first time I saw the movie *E.T.* Almost everyone in the theater cried, including me.

Altered Consciousness

Was I asleep when I saw *E.T.?* ...not at all! Even though my conscious mind realized that a *six-million-dollar puppet* played the role of the extraterrestrial, my subconscious accepted E.T. as a real character. I actually experienced hypnosis (right along with the others in the theater). While I remained very aware of the movie in progress, I tuned out the usually incessant coughing, straw slurping, and throat clearing among theater audiences. Even though I remained fully awake, I definitely experienced an altered state of consciousness.

The word *hypnosis*, coined by an English physician in the 19th century, still gives us an inaccurate impression of trance. Although derived from the Greek word *hypnos*, meaning sleep, hypnosis is not a state of sleep. A better definition might be *altered conscious awareness* (as described above). We may more accurately describe hypnosis as the same relaxed state of mind we enter daily when our brain-wave activity slows down to a frequency called *alpha*. Everyone passes through alpha on the way to and from sleep, so we have all experienced alpha many thousands of times!

Our bodies become physically relaxed during this state of mind, as in meditation, so an observer could perceive us to be asleep. Appearances can be deceiving, however, as a person in hypnosis becomes more aware and/or focused rather than less. With the conscious mind relaxed, the subconscious mind becomes accessible, thus creating expanded possibilities for change. Hollywood leads us to believe that the hypnotist has control; however, the power of control actually resides within the minds of each one of us as we enter hypnosis (as explained more fully later in this chapter). Consequently, all hypnosis could easily be called guided self-hypnosis. I also define hypnosis as guided meditation—or *guided daydreaming*. While professionals still debate to this day over the definition of hypnosis, both my own experience and the experience of many clients validate this definition.

This same state of mental relaxation should already be familiar to you, because the hypnotic state usually occurs when we feel mellow, even though we may not recognize it as hypnosis. We regularly experience four different mental states of mind, which can be measured by an EEG (electroencephalograph).

The Four States of Mind

We remain in the beta state for most of our waking hours. Beta compares to high gear and is a good place for decision making, reasoning, and logic. Brain waves are above 13 cycles per second, often higher, and may or may not be rhythmic.

When our brain waves slow to between 8 and 13 cycles per second, we enter the alpha state of mind. This opens the door between the conscious and subconscious, and it becomes easier to access our memory banks and/or store new information. We also enjoy enhanced creativity and a greater ability to imagine. We also become more suggestible—as Hollywood exploits in movies. Whenever we enter the alpha state—whether guided by a movie, tape, or person—we are technically hypnotized.

Below the two conscious states are theta—the dream state—and delta, which is deep sleep or total unconsciousness. Whether or not you remember your dreams, you must pass through theta on the way to and from delta. Likewise, you must pass through alpha on the way to and from sleep, even if briefly; thus we all experience hypnosis daily!

According to Dr. Barbara B. Brown, author of *Stress and the Art of Biofeedback*, experts vary in their opinions on the exact frequency range of alpha and theta waves. Within a month after my first self-hypnosis book hit the press, a psychologist specializing in the study of brain waves informed me that recent discoveries had indicated that the brain still produces alpha waves even when we are in a total conscious state of beta. At first that bothered me, creating a concern that I might have written incorrect data. A psychiatrist soon clarified that the subconscious mind usually stays in alpha—at walking speed—while the conscious mind jogs along in beta. Then, when we enter hypnosis (or meditation), the conscious slows down to alpha (or walking speed), enhancing communication between the right and left sides of the brain.

Opinions still vary, so I recommend that you draw your own conclusions regarding this debate. In my opinion, it's more important to learn how to make your subconscious become your servant rather than your slave master. This book can help you accomplish that objective by teaching you how to use self-hypnosis effectively. Since I tell my hypnotherapy students that I teach hypnosis as an art rather than as a science, I will also tell all who read this book: *self-hypnosis is an art*. To master the art, you must learn the steps and then *practice* the exercises described in this book.

Who Has the Control?

Before we explore self-hypnosis, let's take a few pages to rip away the Hollywood mysticism from the misrepresented arts of hypnosis and self-hypnosis.

Dr. James Braid, the English physician who coined the word *hypnosis*, eventually admitted that the power is not with the facilitator, but with the person who enters the hypnotic state. Myron Teitelbaum, M.D., author of *Hypnosis Induction Technics*, came to the same conclusion:

> The hypnotist is merely the guide who directs and leads the subject into the trance. (p. 18)

Simply stated, hypnosis does not put you under someone else's power. A female hypnotherapist proved this to me personally when she hypnotized me deeply and tried several different ways to suggest that I shave off my beard. After several minutes of her persistent prejudice, I brought myself out of hypnosis and gave her one lecture on ethics that I hope she remembers for the rest of her life. (Needless to say, I've never allowed her to hypnotize me again!)

Many times my own experience with clients has also proven that the subject, not the hypnotist, retains control. One deepening technique I frequently use involves asking a client to imagine that the left arm feels lighter than air. Yet sometimes, even while definitely in the hypnotic state, clients still reject this suggestion—often just to prove to themselves that choice still exists.

The effective hypnotist does not try to control your mind; he/she serves as an artist who facilitates your ability to use your imagination and respond to simple suggestions. In other words, I do not put a client into trance. The client creates his or her own trance state by using me as a guide, and by allowing my voice to be the point of focus. People often ask, *If this is the case, then why do so many people make spectacles of themselves during stage hypnosis shows?* There are several reasons.

What About Stage Hypnosis?

First, a stage hypnotist often prefaces the show by stating that you cannot be made to do anything against your religious or moral beliefs. If you accept that statement literally before entering hypnosis, then you have just given yourself the autosuggestion that you will do anything else the hypnotist suggests, thus creating the illusion of being under the hypnotist's control!

Another obvious reason for the success of stage hypnosis is people's desire to have a good time. Frequently the volunteers for a stage show know little about hypnosis, but they expect to have fun. Even shy people may enjoy the opportunity to be part of the show while passing the buck to the hypnotist who "gave the suggestion." Most hypnotic volunteers become very creative in carrying out suggestions on stage. It becomes comfortable simply to respond and let the hypnotist be responsible! Most volunteers are aware of audience laughter—and are enjoying it themselves. (At least, such has been my personal experience during the times I have volunteered for participation in stage hypnosis shows.) Some, though, merely follow suggestions even if they do not want to—because they somehow *believe* that they are under the hypnotist's partial control. (Some hypnotists *trick* their subjects into accepting this belief.) These hypnotized people act—or rather, *react*—according to the belief about hypnosis they had before entering that state.

Even during a show, a participant will often reject a suggestion. The stage hypnotist isn't concerned with why someone rejects a group suggestion, but a good entertainer will definitely notice those who do not respond and promptly send them back to their seats in the audience. This inherent threat of rejection leaves an unspoken suggestion: *If you want to stay in the show, do what I say.*

The subject who believes that the hypnotist retains the control responds accordingly; likewise, the participant who knows who has the power will also respond accordingly! Any such participant might initiate the trance termination. In 1991, I saw a woman emerge from deep trance after a suggestion she apparently resented. She gave the stage hypnotist an obscene gesture in front of hundreds of people, and then immediately returned to her seat in the audience.

Occasionally, someone will do things during the show that might feel comfortable only if he/she knows they can be consciously forgotten later—so he/she will then conveniently forget. Even if the hypnotist suggests amnesia, the volunteer can reject that suggestion if desired, but may still pretend to forget while discussing the show with a friend afterward. I mentioned earlier, however, that many people enter hypnosis believing that they are "under the hypnotist's power"—and people tend to get whatever they believe.

I'm not against stage hypnosis when done tastefully; but I am concerned that, in exchange for a few laughs, many stage hypnotists give wrong impressions to people about hypnosis. Hypnotherapy and self-hypnosis sparkle as powerful tools for making the changes we desire in our lives. As a member of National Speakers Association and over the Internet by maintaining the FAQ (Frequently Asked Questions) on the alt.hypnosis newsgroup, I have spent much time and energy to spread greater awareness of the real benefits of hypnotherapy and self-hypnosis. It's time we wake up to the facts of alpha—that state of mind where we all spend so much of our lives.

How We Enter Alpha

We enter the alpha state more often than most people realize. We can be guided into hypnosis by a *thing* as well as by a person. Remember my description of the effect of movies? The average person enters alpha very quickly after getting engrossed in a TV program…

Have you noticed how someone can be perfectly content watching television, only to have a sudden urge to raid the refrigerator during a commercial break? This act demonstrates an hypnotic response to the sponsor's suggestions. Certainly, we can modify or reject the input just as someone in formal hypnosis can reject the hypnotist's suggestions. We might see a pizza commercial and ignore it; but the conscious mind knows where to find a bag of potato chips, so your conscious mind modifies the sponsor's suggestion.

Imagination becomes powerful at such times. If the subconscious produces a brief image of munching potato chips, you can be on your feet in a flash, headed for the kitchen! It's also very easy to check the refrigerator for something else to go with the chips. Does this scenario sound familiar? You demonstrate a response to hypnotic suggestion whenever this occurs—and *television* becomes your hypnotist! A contrary reaction is also possible. For example, I occasionally find myself refusing to buy certain products simply because their commercials insult my intelligence.

Perhaps you will resonate to the next scenario, as do many other parents (or grandparents) of small children. The Saturday morning cartoons can totally mesmerize a child, inducing a deep trance. I have literally stood directly between the child and the TV to gain acceptance of a simple suggestion such as taking a dirty cereal bowl to the kitchen. The young, impressionable mind ignores a parent's suggestion, while accepting the *sponsor's suggestion to get the cereal with the toy enclosed!* Eventually, the response becomes so automatic that the little hand enters the grocery bag, finding and opening the box of cereal—even before the groceries have been put away. I'm certain that I'm not the only parent to witness similar events.

In case you think yourself immune, how often do you remember to ask for Scotch tape, take photocopies, or grab for a facial tissue when you sneeze? For example, what do you think of with the words, *You deserve a break today, at...?*

Another example of our daily trip into the alpha state occurs at night, in bed, just before falling asleep. Have you ever gotten irate at the neighbor's barking dog while you are trying to go to sleep? Some time back my neighbor got a noisy German shepherd, and my bedtime thoughts were: *I can't sleep with that [bleep] dog barking!* After several nights it became apparent that I was giving myself a negative self-hypnotic suggestion to be at the dog's mercy. The resulting insomnia motivated me to reverse the outcome by thinking, *Every sound I hear makes me sleepier and sleepier.* Within one week I developed the ability to sleep soundly with that dog still barking frequently less than thirty feet from my bedroom window!

We can enter alpha in numerous other ways: daydreaming while driving (stay alert), staring out the window while daydreaming, getting lost in a good book, sitting in church engrossed in a sermon, listening to music, or whenever we find our imaginations running freely.

Even hard rock music induces alpha in some people—although not me! Some people believe that music helps them to think well. Looking at the mountains, or lake, or waterfall, or meadow, etc., helps others to think and/or meditate. Remember that alpha enhances memory, creativity, and the ability to imagine. Alpha also increases the subconscious ability to respond to whatever we imagine ourselves doing.

Remember that we may enter alpha at various times during our waking hours and, while there, whatever we imagine goes straight into the subconscious. Let's also remember that we are vulnerable to suggestion, so it behooves us to be careful about whatever we imagine or daydream. Entering a state of meditation, alpha, or self-hypnosis is neither good nor bad; rather, what we think and imagine during trance will produce a positive, neutral, or negative result.

Now let's examine the necessary ingredients for self-hypnosis, or for any successful trance.

Trance Ingredients

Four important mental components help insure the success of a trance: *imagination, belief, expectancy,* and *conviction.* (These trance ingredients are detailed in my hypnosis text, *The Art of Hypnosis: Mastering Basic Techniques,* published by Kendall/Hunt Publishing.) Let's briefly examine them now...

Imagination is the language of the subconscious. You may easily demonstrate this fact by simply imagining your favorite food when you are hungry! A smoker imagining a cigarette soon wants one, especially if trying to quit. A runner imagining exhaustion will quickly tire. A dieter imagining junk food will soon splurge. The exercises at the end of this chapter will help you discover the power of imagination.

Belief adds to the power of imagination. Whatever we believe will happen influences both our imagination and our actions. The ex-smoker who believes he/she will backslide succumbs to intensifying urges. The dieter who believes he/she will successfully reduce will succeed. Belief also applies to self-hypnosis. If you believe it will work, it will! I hope that the realization that *you've already experienced trance* will help you believe in your ability to enter trance at will. If you experience any difficulty believing in your ability to enter self-hypnosis, then I suggest that you practice the exercises in this chapter, several times if necessary, as they will help prepare you for your journey into self-hypnosis.

Expectancy and *conviction* are like twins. If one expects to succeed (or fail), and becomes totally convinced of an expected outcome, that conviction virtually guarantees personal actions that match the expectation. In order to change the expectation, we must first deal with imagination and belief.

Imagination leads to belief (or vice versa), and these both lead to expectation and conviction regardless of the conscious desire—and this principle applies to habits as well as to the state of hypnosis. Building a positive presence of these ingredients creates a greater probability of success.

Let's start the building process with the following mental exercises...

Mental Exercises for Trance Preparation

Stage hypnotists often take a lemon and peel it in front of an audience, pretending to suck the juice. Imagine how you might feel if you saw someone sucking on a lemon. Does your mouth react? Isn't it interesting how we can react to fantasy?

Now enjoy a more *comfortable* exercise. Sit back comfortably in a chair or on a couch. Either have someone read the italic text below, or play back this pre-recorded script:

Stretch your arms out in front of you and close your eyes, and take a deep breath...

(Pause briefly...)

Imagine that a cord is tied to one of your wrists, and a large balloon is tied to the other end of the cord, tugging your arm upward. SEE the balloon and FEEL it tugging...

Now, imagine that you're holding an empty bucket in your other hand, and someone pours water into the bucket. SEE the water pouring, HEAR the water splashing, and FEEL the bucket getting heavier as it gets fuller and fuller... heavier and heavier... pulling your arm down... heavier and heavier, fuller and fuller... as your other arm gets higher and higher...

When you feel obvious movement in one (or both) of the arms, open your eyes. How well did you respond to the above mental exercise? Even a slight movement of one arm indicates the power of your imagination. The conscious mind knows that we are pretending, yet we respond to imagination as though reacting to reality.

Here's another exercise demonstrating our ability to respond to fantasy:

Clasp your hands together, interlacing your fingers. Now extend both index fingers outward, and separate them by about an inch…
     IMAGINE that you have magnets on each fingertip, with opposite poles attracting each other. SEE the magnets, and FEEL the magnetic attraction…

Almost all of my clients respond to at least one of these demonstrations. Sometimes a hypnosis student in my college class refuses to imagine what I suggest, just to test my reaction! My usual response is to put my hand near the blackboard and pretend that I'm going to scratch the blackboard with my fingernails…

Did the sentence in that last paragraph give you a reaction? It's amazing how quickly my students yell out, *Don't do that!*

Even the imaginary scratch on the blackboard demonstrates how we react to imagination. In other words, *imagination is the language of the subconscious.* Practice the exercises of imagination until you find yourself responding to at least one of them. If you need to increase your belief in the power of imagination, simply remember the last time that you saw someone else eating your favorite food. Did it make your mouth water? Consider your emotional responses during a powerful movie. We are moved emotionally because of the power of imagination. Your awareness of how we respond to imagination will help build belief in the power of imagination, an important element of successful self-hypnosis.

When you learn how to take control of your own imagination, self-hypnosis will feel as natural to you as does water to a duck, making self-motivation a more effective tool for establishing positive success habits! Naturally, the two exercises with the above scripts will serve you with the best comfort as you prepare for self-hypnosis. Before you create your own trance, however, let's spend one chapter exploring the history of hypnosis.

Chapter 3

Hypnosis Then and Now

Today we have the freedom to choose hypnotherapy as an agent of change, but events and controversies about trance work may now jeopardize that freedom. Understanding the history of hypnosis may help to calm the controversies and provide greater insight into what might be behind some of them.

Why Explore the History of Hypnosis?

A few readers might wonder why a self-help book includes a chapter on the history of hypnosis. First, I want to satisfy those people who have expressed curiosity about it. If you are one of that group, then enjoy the results of my research (otherwise simply skip to the next chapter). Second, we can gain important insight regarding the still hotly debated question of *who* has the power during a trance. Does the hypnotist have the power, or do we all have the power inside ourselves? We can also benefit from understanding how and why hypnosis still labors under yesterday's misconceptions by giving you greater confidence in your own use of hypnosis, both now and in the future, and whether the trance is self-induced or facilitated by another. Even though one form or another of trance has been used since very early civilization, the true nature of hypnosis seems like a mystery to most people to this day.

The long and often unhappy history of hypnosis demonstrates the importance of the roles of *belief, imagination, expectation,* and *conviction* mentioned in Chapter 2. History also reveals how *ignorance* of these vital trance ingredients resulted in incorrect theories, some of which prevail even now. By glancing at the origin and historical background of some of those early theories of hypnosis, the resulting confusion becomes evident.

The following information comes partly from my own studies, partly from my personal knowledge of certain individuals, and partly from unpublished research notes compiled by Charles Tebbetts and others. I originally wrote a comprehensive overview of trance history in my professional text, *The Art of Hypnosis* (1995, Kendall/Hunt Publishing, permission granted). A condensed version appears here.

Possible Origins of Hypnosis

How old is hypnosis? Many might find it hard to believe, but hieroglyphics found on Egyptian tombs from as early as 3000 B.C. prove that the Egyptians used a form of hypnosis. The Greeks also understood trance, as did the Mayas of South America. Additionally, some hypnotherapists (including me) believe that Jesus induced trance in many whom he healed. Genghis Khan used group suggestion to create hallucinations and motivate his men to fight, demonstrating the value of using a combination of trance and guided imagery to motivate people.

Most people connect trance states with mystic experiences, even though history demonstrates the widespread and successful use of trance for healing and motivation. Why, then, does hypnosis still remain such a mystery today? Contrary to the opinions of some people, we cannot blame Hollywood totally.

First, humans seem selfish by nature. An elite few have jealously guarded the knowledge of trance since the dawn of time, shrouding it in mysticism and religion. Before recorded history, tribal witch doctors and shamans mastered the art of trance, teaching it only to a designated few.

Another reason for the lack of acceptance may also relate directly to human nature: the tendency to fear, ridicule, or turn up our noses at what we don't understand. Consider, for example, how people laughed at the Wright brothers. Most people then thought that if God had intended man to fly, he would have given him wings; now airplanes are a part of life. In the not-too-distant past, many people even labeled electricity a "demonic power."

Should we be surprised that hypnotism, still considered by many to be an occult science, has taken so long to gain recognition and wide-scale acceptance? Even today there is considerable misinformation and ignorance surrounding it, and only in the late 20th century do we find hypnosis emerging as a science as well as an art. Let's now highlight the work of several key pioneers of hypnosis, beginning with perhaps the most famous trance artist of all time.

Franz Anton Mesmer

Hypnotherapists consider Mesmer to be the most famous name in the entire history of hypnosis, even though he never heard of the art or science by that name. This man's work still influences us to this day and thus deserves a detailed overview.

Anton Mesmer was born in Germany in 1734 and studied medicine in Vienna, where he became a practicing physician. As the first man ever to try to explain scientifically what he did, Mesmer became known as the Father of Hypnosis, a title he shares with two other men. (We still speak of "mesmerizing" someone.)

After seeing a demonstration of magnetic cures by Father Maximilian Hell in 1774, Mesmer started experimenting with magnets borrowed from Father Hell. (Can you believe this priest's last name?) Based on these experiments, Mesmer later formulated a theory concerning the influence of planets upon the human body, using it for his doctoral dissertation. He believed that a sort of general magnetic fluid pervaded nature and the human body, and that this fluid had to be evenly distributed throughout the body for wellness. With the magnets, he made "magnetic passes" at his patients, stroking the magnetic field that was alleged to extend several inches from the body. (Now that science has proven the existence of an aura, perhaps we can accept the idea that Dr. Mesmer was ahead of his time.)

Although his theories intrigued many, Mesmer also blended astrology and metaphysics into his theories, thereby damaging whatever credibility he might have had with the skeptics. Eventually they drove him from Vienna to Paris, where the good doctor found new patients to magnetize.

Now let's consider what really happened. Magnets at that time were new and mysterious, and some people *believed* that magnets had great powers. The subject respected this perceived power and became *convinced* that the magnets would produce results. Since people *expected* results, many got them!

Before long, Mesmer discovered that he could help people obtain a "cure" without the magnets. He started "magnetizing" cups of water, and his patients would trance out upon drinking it. He also tied people to magnetized elm trees, and they would immediately go into a trance!

Mesmer's fame grew quickly, and his clinic became a showplace in Paris—where getting *mesmerized* became as popular as going up in hot-air balloons. Mesmer developed the legendary *bacquet*, a large round tub with a seating capacity of about thirty. Holes around the top allowed subjects to reach through and grasp iron rods to receive the "magnetic flow"—to *go with the flow*! The magnetic doctor enhanced the entire scenario with music, unusual lighting, and the presence of highly suggestible subjects, so that even a skeptic generally found it easy to trance out into convulsions by grasping one of the iron rods. A Paris newspaper sent a reporter to debunk Mesmer, but the reporter became a believer instead.

Unfortunately for the evolution of hypnotism, Mesmer *did not know* that his "cures" resulted from his artistry in inducing guided self-trances, helping patients actually use the power of their subconscious for their cures. This lack of knowledge set the stage for a major setback. The skeptics persuaded King Louis XVI to appoint a commission headed by Benjamin Franklin (my great-uncle seven times removed) to investigate Mesmer's work.

Franklin had the good old doctor magnetize a cup of water, which my uncle said he would later give, along with a cup of ordinary water, to a woman. Then my Uncle Ben pulled the old-fashioned *switcheroo*! When the woman drank Mesmer's water, Franklin told her that the water was ordinary, and nothing happened. She then drank from the cup of water that she *believed* to be magnetized, and she *tranced out*. One does not have to be a scientist to realize that the *woman* had the power of trance rather than Dr. Mesmer! Franklin then conducted a similar experiment with a magnetized tree, obtaining similar results. Afterward he stated that Mesmer was a fraud, as all his cures and theatrical results were caused by *imagination*. Any of us could have come to the same conclusion. I wonder if Franklin had any idea that a day would come when an entire profession (hypnotherapy) would rely heavily on his accurate observation!

Had Anton Mesmer really understood the vital role of *belief and imagination*, the entire history of hypnosis would have changed course! Today we know that his patients really experienced *guided self-mesmerism*. Unfortunately for the art of hypnotism, neither Mesmer nor the other pioneers of trance understood who has the power.

Other Hypnosis Pioneers

Father Gassner, a Catholic priest contemporary with Mesmer (1727–1779), worked actively with trance states. Gassner mastered the art of suggestion as a means of faith healing and became perhaps the first of the modern faith healers. He muttered sleep suggestions in Latin while using a diamond-studded cross, sending people into a trance within seconds. As a religious authority, Gassner worked under the most favorable conditions possible for hypnotic response. People believed that he represented God's authority over them, so they expected things to happen when Father Gassner spoke. (Does this sound familiar?) Regardless of whether the cause was human or divine, this priest got results. Many of those he sent into trance got well!

A former student of Mesmer's, Marquis Chastenet de Puysegur (also spelled Pursegur), evolved Mesmer's theories about magnetism. He decided that magnets were not necessary, so he would "magnetize" an elm tree and get results with people visiting that elm tree. Imagine that! The local populace could go enjoy the latest in convulsions even in the Marquis's absence (while he apparently did more important things). Wouldn't you agree that *belief* and *imagination* were at work here? Puysegur duplicated Mesmer's mistake of believing that he was the one with power over his subjects.

John Elliotson, born in 1791, served as a professor of medical theory and practice at University Hospital in London, England. Elliotson discovered that mesmerized patients could undergo major surgery without agony, but the discovery incurred the wrath of his fellow physicians. Elliotson also believed in clairvoyance, so the jealous doctors used this as extra ammunition to put his real work into the same suspect category. The scientific community forced him into retirement, aiming a tragic blow at the leading scientific practitioner of trance.

James Braid (1795–1860), a prominent Scottish surgeon, became famous for coining the word *hypnosis* (derived from the Greek god of sleep, *Hypnos*). His work helped advance hypnosis greatly, but he made one glaring mistake that still impacts it today: he *assumed* that something physiological took place as a result of his fixed-gaze techniques, thereby creating an *absence of volition*. Thus Braid failed to realize that all hypnosis is self-hypnosis. (Some of my peers believe that Braid eventually recognized where the power resides.) The eye-fixation techniques remain to this day, although hypnotherapy currently uses a variety of other methods to guide people into altered states.

James Esdaile (1808–1859), a Scottish doctor, used hypnosis in surgery with astounding results. While working in India, he performed several thousand minor operations and about three hundred major ones, including nineteen amputations, all painlessly. Due mostly to the removal of postoperative shock through hypnosis, he cut the 50% mortality rate of that time down to less than 8%! (One book even reported less than 5%.) When he returned home, however, Esdaile failed to duplicate those results he tried to use scientists as his subjects; and they resisted hypnosis because of their personal skepticism. Again, this demonstrates the power of belief and indicates who has the real power of trance!

In the late 19th century, two doctors, Ambroise Liebault and Hippolite Bernheim, established a school of hypnotism in Nancy, France. They also believed that the physician had the power rather than the patient. Concurrently, Dr. James Martin Charcot set up a hypnosis school at Salpetriere. Dr. Charcot became the first one to identify and label the various levels of hypnotic depth, giving scientific names that we still use today. But like the other pioneers of trance, he also misunderstood where the power really is, yet nonetheless obtained many good results. Apparently many of his cures were permanent. And then along came Freud...

Hypnosis Regresses

Sigmund Freud studied hypnotism at both the Nancy and Salpetriere schools. According to Billa Zanuso, author of *The Young Freud*, Freud did not believe that deep levels of hypnosis were necessary for change; rather, he taught that suggestions could be accepted and past events recalled even in a light state of hypnosis. Unfortunately for the future of hypnotherapy, Freud apparently was not skilled in trance induction. He admitted that he wearied quickly of the "monotony of the sleep suggestions."

When working with one patient, Freud failed to induce a hypnotic trance. He almost reached the point of despair when, in desperation, he hit on the idea of trying free association in the waking state. When the case proved to be successful, Freud apparently welcomed the opportunity to drop hypnosis from his methods. He created and publicized the technique of *psychoanalysis* and then led a general abandonment of the use of hypnosis.

Despite the advances in the use of hypnotism made by others, Freud's failure managed to push hypnosis backward, leaving only a flickering flame of interest behind.

The Most Common Mistake of the Pioneers

You will have noticed that these accounts all have a common thread: all the researchers believed that *they* held the power—that the people experimented upon gave up their free will and subjected themselves to the operator (hence the word *subject*). This common opinion is confirmed by some of today's researchers of hypnosis (and is still debated by a few).

If any of our pioneers, particularly Freud, had understood all the trance ingredients, they might have come to the conclusion that all hypnosis is guided self-hypnosis and the history of both hypnotism and psychology would have been forever altered! Instead, the 20th century dawned with hypnosis back virtually in the Dark Ages. But by the end of this century an amazing evolution in hypnosis was taking place.

20th-century Hypnosis

During the time between Freud's discoveries and World War I, only the efforts of a few interested men kept hypnosis from vanishing entirely. Of these, the brightest name is Emile Coue's.

Coue made some lasting contributions to the art of self-hypnosis, especially with his theories of waking hypnosis and autosuggestion, by taking a totally new and innovative approach. He explained the law of conflict that I briefly mentioned in the first chapter, calling it "will and imagination." In *Self-Mastery Through Conscious Autosuggestion*, he stated:

> This will that we claim so proudly, always yields to the imagination. It is an absolute rule that admits of no exception.

'Blasphemy! Paradox!' you will exclaim. 'Not at all! On the contrary, it is the purest truth,' I shall reply....

Suppose that we place on the ground a plank 30 feet long by 1 foot wide. It is evident that everybody will be capable of going from one end to the other of this plank without stepping over the edge. But now change the conditions of the experiment, and imagine this plank placed at the height of the towers of a cathedral. Who then will be capable of advancing even a few feet along this narrow path? (p. 7)

This explanation of the law of conflict remains a very significant contribution by Coue, because he apparently realized where the power resides! To this day, many hypnotherapists use various metaphors to illustrate the law of conflict; I wonder how many trance artists realize that Coue gave us this important contribution. Personally, I consider him to be the *father of self-hypnosis* because of his important work with autosuggestion.

While a few others made contributions in the early 20th century, perhaps the entertainers and masters of stage hypnosis have done more than most people realize to keep the flames of interest flickering through entertaining public demonstrations.

After World War I, trauma caused by the anxiety of war brought about an acute need for a fast method of therapy. In desperation, the medical profession turned to hypnosis. Again, during World War II, the medical applications of hypnosis surged. Dave Elman helped the upswing by teaching hypnosis to many in the medical profession. Then, in 1958, the Council on Mental Health of the American Medical Association finally accepted the use of hypnosis.

Among the 20th-century scientific researchers of hypnosis, one name shines brilliantly above all others: Milton Erickson, M.D. He became recognized as the most important contributor to the acceptance both of the medical uses of hypnotism and of the art of hypnotherapy. Dr. Erickson, often called the *grandfather of hypnotherapy*, forever changed its history. People with outstanding professional credentials have examined, analyzed, and written books about his work, and all professional hypnotherapists recognize and respect it.

The *Art* of Hypnotherapy: Birth of a New Profession

The seeds planted by Dr. Erickson's vitally important work grew into the *art* of hypnotherapy, giving rise to a profession composed of men and women dedicated to using hypnotherapy to help people improve their lives. They use hypnosis for many non-medical objectives—such as motivation, habit control, etc. Countless numbers of clients validate its benefits, such as the hundreds of thousands of former smokers who have successfully quit smoking through the use of hypnosis.

With a professional referral, many professional hypnotherapy artists can also employ hypnosis for medical purposes such as pain management. Increasing numbers of physicians, psychiatrists, and psychologists refer patients to hypnotherapists; ethical hypnotherapists who know their limitations refer clients to other professionals when necessary. I hope to see this cooperation increase.

Dr. Bernie Siegel, M.D., promoted hypnotherapy in his book, *Love, Medicine & Miracles*:

A hypnotherapist can be valuable in the beginning, especially if the patient has trouble entering the state of deep relaxation. No matter who sets the course for the first meditative sessions—doctor, counselor, hypnotherapist, or the patient...(p. 230)

Hypnosis is skyrocketing as a profession, enjoying more popularity than at any time in history. Numerous state and national professional hypnotherapy associations have sprung up in recent years, both in United States and internationally. These associations promote hypnotherapy as a career for people who wish to devote themselves *full-time* to its practice. *The United States Dictionary of Occupation Titles* defines hypnotherapist as a separate profession. Perhaps for the first time in recorded history, the art of trance induction is available to anyone seriously interested in becoming a student.

The legitimate hypnotherapy profession has produced its own superstars. People such as Ormond McGill and Charles Tebbetts have already become legends and are considered *masters of the art*. Ormond McGill traveled the world performing stage hypnosis during much of the 20th century and has written numerous books on hypnotism and meditation. Prior to his death, Charles Tebbetts became a master teacher of hypnotherapy. He has been recognized for lifetime achievement by the International Hypnosis Hall of Fame, which was established in the last decade to recognize and preserve the work of the stars of hypnosis from both the scientific community and the hypnotherapy profession.

Legal Recognition of Hypnotherapy

What I believe will go down in history as one of the biggest breakthroughs for the hypnotherapy profession came in 1987 in Washington state, which legally recognized hypnotherapy as a profession with its own code of professional ethics that hypnotherapists and counselors alike must observe.

Most recently, Indiana passed legislation, effective July 1, 1997, requiring hypnotherapists to have at least 350 hours of training. Other states may eventually pass similar legislation. While some hypnotherapists believe this training standard to be too high, the required hours are less than the requirements of other professions. Many hypnotherapists fear legislation, but licensure and/or registration, combined with training standards, apply to other health care professions. Unfortunately for hypnotherapy, however, not all laws contribute constructively to the profession.

In a strange twist of historical repetition, some of the worst criticism of professional hypnotherapists comes from the *very same psychological and medical communities researching and advocating the scientific uses of hypnotism!* A select few call us "lay hypnotists" and are spending time and money in efforts to give themselves the exclusive legal right to control hypnosis. Hypnotherapists in Texas woke up one morning in 1995 to find their livelihoods legislated out of existence! A legislative change in the legal definition of the practice of psychology made it illegal for even a *well-trained veteran hypnotherapist* to practice in Texas. Meanwhile, a *licensed mental health counselor* could practice hypnosis merely after taking a three-day course, or even if only self-taught in the art of trance! Were similar regulations imposed throughout the country, you could find it difficult to find any hypnotherapist available to teach you self-hypnosis.

In many ways this conflict resembles the years-long war between the AMA and chiropractors. Chiropractors are here to stay, as the *public deserves the freedom to choose alternative health care*. Both the scientific community and hypnotherapists must find ways to enhance the level of communication between them and to increase mutual cooperation if hypnotherapy is to remain alive.

If we are to have legislation, then let it serve both the public and the hypnotherapy profession. The public must be allowed to retain freedom of choice.

The Future of Hypnosis

In spite of our professional growing pains, increasing numbers of people with medical backgrounds and other advanced degrees support the various professional hypnotherapy organizations, working to help promote hypnotherapy in a way that will finally bring trance work out of the Dark Ages once and for all. The future of hypnosis finally looks bright enough to grow to its full potential, and perhaps hypnotherapy will finally attain total enlightenment!

Chapter 4

Entering Self-hypnosis

Now that you have read about the alpha state, are you ready to experience it?

The first self-hypnosis exercise, called *progressive relaxation*, represents only one of thousands of methods of entering an alpha state. If you have learned another method from another book or from a seminar, use what you prefer as long as your chosen method works.

I suggest you read through this exercise once or twice to become familiar with the contents before you begin using the actual technique. The specific words you use can vary from the typical session suggested here, but you should follow the basic format.

Progressive Relaxation

Now let's begin the session. Find a comfortable place to recline or lie down. If you wear hard contact lenses, remove them. If you chew gum, throw it away. Also, be certain that your clothing feels comfortable. If possible, unplug your phone or turn on your answering machine—and make certain to put your pets in another room. Some animals seem to sense the mental peace you feel in the alpha state and will want to be close. (Experience taught me that a cat suddenly pouncing on my stomach during relaxation could be quite a jolt!)

Now that you're comfortable, take several deep breaths. Close your eyes if you wish. Imagine yourself letting go of all of your cares and tensions as easily as you let go of the air from your lungs.

Background music is optional—but recommended if you meditate in an area where there may be distracting outside noise.

Think to yourself words like the italics on the following pages while fantasizing about being in a peaceful place like a beach, the woods, a waterfall, lake, stream, meadow, etc. Note that the grammar is often imperfect, because the words are intended for the subconscious. Three dots indicate a pause...

As I now imagine a relaxing sensation entering my toes, my breathing continues to be free and easy—just as when I sleep. The relaxation becomes more and more real with each breath I take, moving up into my feet...

It feels soooooo good to relax that it becomes easy, comfortable, and automatic for the relaxation to move up into my ankles... The relaxing sensation becomes more and more real with each breath I take. It now moves up into my calves. All my nerves and muscles just let go, responding to my desire to relax... The relaxation moves right on through my knees, going up into my thighs... all the nerves and muscles letting go into a deeper and deeper state of relaxation.

My hips relax. It feels soooooo good to relax, that the feeling continues right on into my stomach muscles and up around my rib cage.

With each breath I go deeper and deeper relaxed. The relaxation moves on into my lower back, going right up into my shoulders—just as though gentle fingers have just given me a soothing back rub. The soothing feeling of relaxation moves down through my elbows, going right on out through my hands and fingers… With each breath I take, I just go deeper and deeper…

The back of my neck relaxes… My scalp relaxes… It feels soooooo good to relax that the feeling of soothing comfort moves into my forehead and temples. With each breath I just go deeper and deeper. My cheeks relax. My jaw muscles relax… My entire body now feels completely relaxed…

At this point you may very well be in a light or medium state of alpha consciousness from this sample induction. If you practice self-hypnosis at night before going to sleep, you may find yourself sound asleep long before you finish the exercise. Some of my clients tend to fall asleep before getting past their knees. If you still feel considerable awareness, however, you may wish to deepen the relaxation by using additional self-talk as follows:

As I now count from ten down to one, I become deeper and deeper relaxed with each number—just drifting down into a very soothing tranquillity.
Number ten—deeper and deeper, relaxing physically…
Number nine—deeper and deeper, relaxing mentally…
Number eight—deeper and deeper, relaxing emotionally…
Number seven—deeper and deeper, relaxing totally…
Number six—every nerve and muscle relaxes completely…
Number five—each number taking me deeper and deeper…
Number four—the deeper I go, the easier it is to go deeper…
Number three—just drifting into total relaxation…
Number two—just drifting into deeeeep hypnotic peace…
Number one—waaaaaaaaaaaaay down deep…

Again, some people may benefit by also fantasizing about a peaceful place with pleasant sights, sounds, and feelings. Others may prefer to use the script as written, without the added "safe place." Make your own choice. If you prefer, you can record this script into a tape player, changing all the "I" and "my" words into the second person.

You may experience time distortion—finding that time seems to condense or expand (ten minutes seems like two, or twenty). Also, you may notice that your mind tends to wander. In fact, your thoughts may wander considerably as you go deeper into the alpha state. You may have to keep bringing yourself back to each new number, sometimes forgetting the last number counted. If this happens, just go on with the first number that comes to your mind. You may have to count down twice to get deeper, or count from a higher number. Many people start the countdown with twenty—and some even start with one hundred. You make the choice.

You may return to full beta awareness by simply telling yourself that you will feel wonderful and wide-awake at the count of five. Then count from one to five either mentally or out loud. If you wish, use the following script as a guide…

Now, I am going to count from one up to five and then I am going to say "fully aware." At the count of five, my eyelids open and I feel calm, refreshed, relaxed, fully aware, and normal in every way.

One... Slowly, calmly, easily, and gently returning to full awareness once again.

Two... Each muscle and nerve in my body is loose, limp, and relaxed, and I feel wonderfully good.

Three... From head to toe I am feeling perfect in every way... physically perfect, mentally alert, and emotionally serene... and when I get behind the wheel of your vehicle, I am totally alert in every way, responding appropriately to any and all traffic situations.

Number four... My eyes begin to feel sparkling clear, just as though they were bathed in fresh spring water. On the next number now, my eyelids open and I am then calm, rested, refreshed, fully aware, and feeling good in every way.

Number five... Eyelids open now. I am fully aware once again.

Take a deep breath, fill up your lungs, and stretch.

While some clients find that they can enjoy progressive relaxation during the first attempt, most others find that they must practice the technique several times first. A minority of clients may discover the need for a different technique; so you may be asking an important question: *What if I don't respond to progressive relaxation?* I can best answer that question by providing additional options...

Alternate Exercises

A minority of people may find their patience wearing thin trying to enter self-hypnosis with the technique described above. Although you certainly have the option of choosing a hypnotherapist to help you, one of the following alternate inductions may work better for you...

Eye Fixation

Get comfortably seated, reclined, or lying down. Stare at an object, such as a candle or a dim light. A candle works well, because the flickering produces eye fatigue (although you may use any object if your eyes are sensitive to light). Take two or three very deep breaths before you begin. Now stare at your chosen object, and imagine your eyelids are getting heavier and heavier with each breath you take. Say to yourself...

As I try to keep my eyes focused on the candle [light, or other object], my eyelids become heavier, droopy, and drowsy... The harder I try to keep my eyes open, the more they want to close... As I breathe deeply and slowly, my entire body just wants to relax and let go... relax and let go... until my eyes just want to close all by themselves...

Repeat this until you find your eyes getting so tired that they have to close. Once your eyes finally close, continue with the deepening described in the Progressive Relaxation script.

This eye-fixation technique works well as an alternative for some who might fail to respond to progressive relaxation. A Boeing employee told me some years ago that he could stare at a candle and simultaneously imagine his arm feeling lighter than air. Within seconds his arm floated in an apparent weightless feeling. He demonstrated his ability in my office, putting himself into a rather deep trance within one minute. Naturally, his ability made my work much easier! He combined eye fixation with a variation on mental misdirection, discussed next...

Mental Misdirection

Some hypnotherapists use the imagination to create a physical response, misdirecting conscious attention in order to produce a trance. You can do this for yourself by taking one of the exercises described in Chapter 2 and holding the imaginary water bucket a little longer.

Get comfortably seated or reclined. Now hold your arms up in front of you and imagine the bucket and balloons as mentioned in the earlier exercise of imagination.

I now imagine that a cord is tied to my wrist, and a hundred helium balloons are tied to the other end of the cord, tugging my arm upward. I can SEE the balloons and FEEL them tugging...

I'm holding an empty bucket in the other hand, and someone pours water into the bucket. I can SEE the water pouring, HEAR the water splashing, and FEEL the bucket getting heavier as it gets fuller and fuller... heavier and heavier... pulling my arm down... heavier and heavier, fuller and fuller... as my other arm gets higher and higher...

As the bucket gets heavier and fuller, my arm just wants to release the bucket as I release myself into trance... The harder I try to hold up the bucket, the heavier it gets...until I release the bucket and release myself into trance... When I release the bucket, my arm drops and I just drop off into deep, hypnotic peace... or I can release myself into total relaxation...

If you feel responsive to your imagination by now, you can drop both arms down and proceed with the counting as described earlier in this chapter; otherwise continue...

Someone DOUBLES the number of helium balloons, while someone else drops a rock into my bucket... The bucket is getting SO HEAVY that it would be so easy to just release the bucket and release myself into trance... It's so easy to release the bucket and just release myself into trance...

Drop your arms into your lap now, and proceed with the counting previously described for deepening your trance. Use the awakening technique described above when you are ready to return to beta consciousness.

Very few of my clients use mental misdirection to enter self-hypnosis, but some of my students report satisfying results. You may wish to try several times each of the techniques described in this chapter, and then choose the one you like the best.

Personal Observations...

Some people drift off to sleep practicing self-hypnosis, so be sure to set an alarm unless you have time for a nap!

Many people remain very aware and start noticing distracting sounds or distracting physical feelings, such as uncomfortable clothing or an itch. When you enter a light state of alpha, you have an *increased awareness* of anything perceived through the five senses. Rather than thinking that you might not be in hypnosis because of hearing background noise, etc., recognize your increased awareness as a signal that you have already reached a light trance state!

If the counting fails to deepen you to your satisfaction, you may try other helpful techniques that involve additional use of your imagination. For example, you can use an imaginary elevator to help you go deeper or, if you don't like elevators, use an escalator, slide, or steps. You could also be floating into a cloud, walking into the woods, lying on a beach listening to waves, or you may be getting into an imaginary Jacuzzi. (Note: DO NOT do this exercise while sitting in a real Jacuzzi!) Another deepening technique involves adding a *peaceful place* to the meditation. Again, you may incorporate these deepening techniques in any of the induction exercises described in this chapter. (A later chapter contains an empowerment exercise to help you enjoy your peaceful place.)

The degree of success varies from person to person. Some of you may find that the progressive relaxation technique works well the very first time. Others may have to practice all the above techniques (as I did) until the best one is found. In fact, I had so much stress when I first tried self-hypnosis that I had to go to a hypnotherapist for posthypnotic suggestion to help me learn self-hypnosis. Even simple meditation had proven difficult previously, because others instructed me to simply "blank out" my mind. Well, that's difficult at best, if not almost impossible, for me to do because, even when I relax, my mind still runs a thousand miles per second. (That's why I create my own safe place when relaxing. You may find a benefit in doing the same.)

Practice entering self-hypnosis through each of the exercises in this chapter at least once before attempting any of the other self-hypnosis exercises in this book. As you develop your ability to relax, you may find yourself able to enter an alpha state easily by taking two or three deep breaths and thinking the word *relax* each time you exhale. Numerous clients create what they call a centering technique to help them enter the alpha state more easily each time; some of my students refine their centering into a signal for quickly entering the alpha state. Employing such a trigger for instant self-hypnosis has many benefits.

If you feel you need help, find a qualified hypnotherapist in your area to work with you. (Refer to the questions and answers section in the Appendix for tips on finding a qualified hypnotherapist.) If you wish, you may record any of the above scripts on a cassette tape and *listen* to the suggestions to relax. If you prefer this method, remember to change the "I am" to the "you are" format rather than keeping the first-person format.

Good luck!

Part Two

Subconscious
Programming

Chapter 5

Why Program the Subconscious?

What do motivational seminars and New Year's resolutions have in common? Most people forget them by the following week. Why? We may set ambitious goals, but the desire to change often exists only at the conscious level. Remember the law of conflict discussed in Chapter 1? In a battle between the conscious and subconscious, the subconscious invariably wins because our minds resemble computers.

Our Mental Computer

A computer terminal accepts input, and the computer gives output. In order to change the output, we must either change the input or change the program. This holds true for the subconscious mind. When we try to change a habit pattern or a way of thinking by simply changing the input without changing the subconscious program, replaying the original program triggers the old habit pattern. In life, it is often easier to change the program than it is to permanently change the input.

For example, a friend of mine left the country for an extended period of time. She decided to stop smoking and simply did not buy any more cigarettes. Two months after returning home, while having a cup of coffee she unintentionally picked up a friend's lit cigarette. The old input of the smoking trigger resulted in a subconscious response based on old program tapes. My friend believed she had "blown it" and consequently started smoking two packs a day almost immediately.

Several diet counselors have told me that 97% of people who pay money to lose weight regain all the lost pounds in less than two years! In other words, *diets work on the body but not the mind.* Unless we change the subconscious program tapes, willpower works only for a short time—and the dieter almost always backslides. The temporary input of the diet counselor may cause temporary changes, but, when one returns to the old input, the behavior corresponds to the previous subconscious programming. The sight of favorite foods frequently triggers the desire to backslide. Friends can also blow the dieter's best intentions by helping to execute the old program tapes. In my business, we refer to subconscious programming as "old tapes" since our minds retain everything. Some therapists prefer the terms *anchoring* and *triggers.* Both are correct.

Anchoring and Triggers

Anchoring is the act of *programming* subconscious tapes. The *trigger* is the signal that plays the old tape, or *executes the program*. Many therapists today utilize anchoring and triggers to help clients gain empowerment; I do, too. Triggers influence much of what we do every day of our lives. Let me explain further.

Do you need to think about every step when tying your shoes? Your conscious sends a quick signal to your brain that triggers your subconscious into action. How about opening a door? We do this automatically; yet a parent often laughs a lot observing his/her small child learning how to open doors for the first time. We find ourselves subconsciously stopping at red lights, braking and accelerating automatically, picking up the phone and answering appropriately whether at work or home; that is, doing many small tasks on "autopilot."

Can you relate to most of these examples? Our mental tapes influence our actions, whether at home or work, in sports or in social circumstances. This is true whether we are alone or with others. For the most part, I consider it a blessing that we can learn to respond automatically to triggers, because doing so makes doing many of life's mundane chores much simpler by freeing our minds to think about whatever else we choose.

The specific reaction triggered by activating an old tape depends on the program previously anchored to the trigger. Repetition over time usually provides the subconscious anchor to a trigger. Contrary to what some people believe, however, triggers sometimes become anchored suddenly, such as during an intense emotional experience or an hypnotic trance.

Because nature dislikes a vacuum, when I am trying to help a client change old habits I recommend replacing the undesired reaction with a new response. For example, one deep breath of air in response to a light-up trigger has no calories and no side effects. Frequent snackers can substitute water for snacks.

Certain events can trigger desires (or urges) as well, such as a smoking urge. The mere act of passing a vending machine often triggers the smoking urge, so someone who smokes may be vulnerable to smoking without consciously deciding to light up. Dieters might immediately desire to eat something sweet upon seeing someone else eat candy. We might prefer to call this *temptation*; regardless of the definition, our mental computer responds to old tapes anchored (programmed) in the past.

We can also anchor emotions in the mind, or use emotion to make a trigger more powerful. When an emotional event anchors a tape into the subconscious, the same emotions can easily be surfaced by any type of trigger that reminds the subconscious of the same event. Phobias provide evidence of anchoring emotions. For example, a vicious dog attack could easily make a child become afraid of dogs for many years. Later, the mere sight of a dog triggers fear in that person, even into adulthood. Good emotions can also become anchored into the mind. It becomes beneficial to rehearse desired events in your imagination during self-hypnosis and to fantasize good emotions while establishing (or anchoring) a trigger.

While many of our subconscious tapes are beneficial, the question remains: how do we deal with undesired triggers or tapes?

"Old Tapes" Can Be Changed

Unfortunately, we can't just erase a program tape. Instead, we must record a new program tape over the old one, replacing it. Had my friend changed the response to the old smoking trigger to a deep breath instead of a light up, her chances of long-term success would have been better. Instead, she tried to delete the response altogether, yet eventually resurfaced her old smoking reaction.

Some old tapes relate to attitudes. We may be programmed to say *thank you* when appropriate and act according to certain social standards. We accept these good-attitude tapes without thinking about them. Other attitude tapes enter our minds as well, such as *I have my father's temper*, or *I'm lousy with math*, or *All my relatives are overweight, it runs in the family.*

One important fact deserves emphasis here: once opened, the subconscious mind does not permit us to keep program tapes blank. Either *you* remain in control of your own programming, or you end up turning control over to somebody or something else. This seems even more true with attitude tapes. For example, dieters often have ups and downs with weight because others influence them subconsciously. (Some people call this the *yo-yo effect.*) I've seen clients get stressed, only to use food to stuff the stress into the subconscious. Because of the impact negative remarks from a friend or relative have on attitude or self-esteem, smokers trying to quit frequently backslide after hearing them. Have you ever given someone else the power to influence your tapes?

Some people have the ability to let other people's opinions roll off them like water off of a duck's back. Most of us, however, occasionally seem to be vulnerable to negative input from relatives or people whom we consider close. Such negativity seeps into the subconscious much more quickly whenever we do not actively maintain control our of our own minds!

During my time as a sales manager, one man in my unit was always revved up after attending an inspiring motivational seminar. He would make several sales calls and close a sale, only to take a tailspin into a slump at the first sign of criticism. My consistently good producer believed in success at a subconscious level and programmed herself to release a poor prospect to go on to a better one. The first sales rep worked twice as many hours too, getting only half the results! Both had equal talent and ability, but they got dramatically different results!

Any athlete experiencing extended bad luck demonstrates how the mind influences results. If a baseball player believes he/she will make an out, that out usually gets recorded. Watch a bowler who believes that he/she has fallen victim to a slump, and the ball just seems to keep missing the right pins. Golf is a prime example of using mind over matter—the matter being the club and ball! Just fantasize where you do NOT want the ball to go, and watch how often the club seems to know how to hit the ball into that dreaded location. (I speak from personal experience with golf!)

Attitude has a profound impact on the subconscious, so we must do whatever possible to avoid playing negative-attitude tapes. When the subconscious mind gets filled with negative triggers or program tapes, we have great difficulty staying in a positive frame of mind, unless we change those tapes at the subconscious level. We must decide which tapes need changing and then begin *replacing* them with new programs. What's needed, then, is a simple way to accomplish this goal. Additionally, the subconscious must accept the new programs in order for us to stay motivated and realize permanent habit change. My own professional experience proves that this process involves more than visualization alone and more than affirmations alone.

I have successfully taught people this process for years, both in private sessions and business seminars. The key to success lies in mastering *self-hypnosis for empowerment*, and building upon what I've presented so far. The remaining chapters provide step-by-step instructions, but we first need to understand the five methods of subconscious programming that are explained in the next chapter.

Chapter 6

Gateways to the Subconscious

According to my late mentor, Charles Tebbetts, there are five basic ways to change our subconscious programming. He discussed them thoroughly in his hypnosis course and summarized them in his book, *Self-Hypnosis and Other Mind Expanding Techniques*. I suggest that you memorize these five gateways to motivating the subconscious: repetition, authority, desire for identity (ego), hypnosis, and emotion.

While I believe in the value of mastering self-hypnosis, I also give clients a variety of other tools to use to achieve their goals. Over the years, I've devoted considerable time to developing a workable approach to using these five gateways, or subconscious motivators, for habit control. You may already recognize some of these methods as familiar ways of effecting a change. Used alone, each gateway has a chance to succeed if there is little or no opposing input. Used harmoniously, these five motivators open wide the doors of subconscious motivation to help you implement your conscious desire for change. Let's examine them now.

Gateway #1: Repetition

Metaphorically speaking, we walk slowly on a dirt path through Gateway #1.

How often have you heard that practice makes perfect? Everyone knows that you can learn a new habit by practicing. The piano teacher insists on practicing scales; the baseball coach insists on batting practice; the elementary-school teacher drills students on multiplication tables. Any skill improves with practice. Repetition does work but takes time. The amount of time can vary from person to person based on other subconscious beliefs as well as on an individual's natural and/or developed ability.

While repetition can create a new habit pattern or way of thinking, have you ever tried to delete an old habit by the repetition of avoidance? Many people riding a bicycle for the first time in years seem surprised at their ability to stay balanced! The subconscious still remembers this skill, as well as all learned habits. These habits can be *replaced*, but not easily erased.

If you find that difficult to believe, again consider the smoking habit. Numerous resolutions to quit smoking literally go up in smoke! For example, the smoker I mentioned in the last chapter simply tried to delete an old habit by ignoring old smoking triggers. She did avoid buying cigarettes, but the subconscious patterns remained dormant, waiting to be activated once again. Over time, the old smoking triggers had become strongly anchored in her subconscious. Consequently, when a situation occurred that used to trigger her light-up urge, she immediately grabbed her friend's lit cigarette without even consciously realizing what she had done!

This same principle holds true for dieters who swallow their best intentions along with their junk food. Whether the food trigger is the vending machine at work, or simply eating junk food as a response to seeing another person indulge, old responses tend to linger. Common smoking triggers are: turning a key in an ignition, picking up a beverage, walking through the front door, etc. Common weight triggers are: seeing food, seeing a vending machine, TV commercials, etc.

Sometimes repetition can help you can replace an old habit with a new one. If repetition alone does not work, however, some subconscious resistance may be working against you; if so, you must use more than repetition alone to replace the undesired habit. Now let's find out why, and take a look at the more powerful ways of reaching the subconscious.

Gateway #2: Authority

Suggestions or commands presented by an authority figure often go straight into the subconscious (even from impersonal authority, such as proven laws of health). Such statements will either push an "obey" button or create a desire to rebel. Ideas or concepts taught by someone in authority often impact the subconscious and can be seen more easily in children than in adults. Third graders, for example, may believe anything that "Teacher says." If the teacher tells a child that he/she excels in math, the compliment motivates the student to do well.

Because of childhood programming by authority figures, some people with severe weight problems often clean their plates automatically even though they are not hungry.

During my original training in advanced hypnotherapy, I watched a videotaped regression of an engineer whose fifth-grade teacher had told him that he couldn't spell. The boy's mother then reinforced the new belief, and he had spent the next thirty years of his life spelling no better than the average fourth grader. Two authority figures had programmed him to believe that he did not have the ability to spell well; that belief remained until he finally released it and allowed his subconscious to receive positive beliefs about his spelling ability. Within a month, he started spelling as well as the average adult.

Because of repeated negative comments about salesmen uttered by their parents, in later life sales people often face difficulties making prospecting calls. Smokers sometimes smoke because their parents told them to wait until adulthood; after reaching maturity, they lit up.

Perhaps you can remember certain ideas presented by your parents and teachers. As adults, we may feel less vulnerable to new subconscious programming by authority figures. Neither our parents nor our former teachers and college instructors now run our lives, but the power that they once held over us can still exert tremendous impact in certain situations.

Certain current authority or authority-wannabes (such as: deity, individual [employer, minister, professional authority], organization [government], or non-entity [laws of health] may also directly impact the subconscious, creating an immediate "obey" or "rebel" response. Some teenagers rebel against authority by smoking; some smokers find difficulty quitting because they resent being told by employers not to smoke. I've had clients tell me that their smoking actually *increased* when their doctors told them to quit. In short, we sometimes have an illogical desire to do something simply because an authority figure forbids it. We may also find ourselves rebelling if a *would-be authority* tries to force us to abide by his/her opinions—such as a stranger telling someone to put out a lighted cigarette.

One such example happened to a very dear friend of mine with whom I worked during the 1970s. Any time someone even *hinted* that he shouldn't smoke, he argued for smokers' rights and lit up at the first opportunity. He smoked for over twenty years; while he tried to quit, he failed. He finally just decided to go on enjoying the habit. (Of course, this happened before my professional entry into hypnotherapy!)

After surgery for a collapsed lung, his doctor came into the hospital room and said: *If you want to live longer than six months, throw your cigarettes away!* My friend respected the doctor as a medical authority, so his subconscious totally opened Gateway #2 for any health-related suggestions from the doctor. From then on, my friend remained a nonsmoker, for over ten years, until the day he died!

Of course, when we give credibility to an outside authority, negative programming can be implanted just as easily as positive programming. The subconscious doesn't know the difference between right and wrong. Rather, the subconscious merely accepts whatever the conscious mind allows to enter. So monitor what goes into your mind!

Common *positive* authority motivators for smoking cessation AND weight control are: health benefits, medical advice, prayer. Common *negative* motivators are: desire to rebel, past painful encounter with authority figure, compulsion to clean the plate (weight control only). Your own attitudes determine whether you have a dirt road or a paved road through Gateway #2.

Gateway #3: Desire for Identity (Ego)

Whether we like it or not, we have an ego that craves belonging, acceptance, recognition, and love. My late mentor called this motivator "Desire for Identity." I prefer to refer to this subconscious gateway simply as the ego. It opens to several avenues:

Peer Pressure

All of us have experienced the power of peer pressure.

How many parents have heard your children beg you for a particular style of clothing merely because other kids at school already wear that style? When my son turned eighteen, he felt that he needed $50 jeans instead of $25 jeans of like quality (a different brand name) simply because of concern over the opinions of his classmates.

Children can do very illogical and dangerous things simply because of a "dare" from a sibling or a friend. The scene from the movie *Stand by Me* in which young boys run across a train bridge gave me an instant hypnotic regression to childhood! My cousin had dared me to walk across a similar bridge, and an oncoming train made it a life-threatening situation. Had I been four inches closer, my life would have ended right then. That dare was the last one I ever accepted from my cousin.

How many smokers started the habit because of peer pressure? Most of my clients wishing to quit smoking list peer pressure as the reason they started in the first place. These clients originally bought into the *identity of a smoker* because of their friends and/or their perceptions of adulthood.

We can justify peer pressure because of youth, right? Does age close this gateway to the subconscious?

To answer that question, consider how many billions of dollars the cosmetics industry and fashion designers earn by catering to the desire to look good! Lest you men think that applies only to women, what about our habit of dressing in a long-sleeved shirt, coat, and tie on a 95-degree day? On one hand, it's absurd to be uncomfortable and inappropriately dressed for the weather; yet I personally choose to buy into the peer pressure of wearing a business suit because I feel more accepted, especially during a public-speaking engagement. A friend of mine, a state senator, appeared in the legislature on a hot day in a short-sleeved shirt. Other legislators asked him to go home and dress properly! These lawmakers chose custom over comfort, even though discomfort risked clouding their legislative judgment. Perhaps someday tens of millions of businessmen will get wise and change an outdated tradition. Until then, we will continue to be hot and uncomfortable by overdressing on summer days—yet justify our actions because of a subconscious acceptance of tradition! Those who attempt to change first will be criticized and judged by those who still cling to the old subconscious programming.

Mentor

We love to admire heroes. Many celebrities relish this fact and enjoy receiving huge sums of money from sponsors who recognize our need for mentors.

People of all ages emulate sports heroes. While umpiring a little league baseball game years ago, I wiped a teenager's spit from my face while he was at bat. When I asked him why he needed to spit, he said he wanted to be just like his favorite baseball player.

When we choose to emulate a friend, sports hero, or movie star, we tend to soak up that person's habits and mannerisms like a sponge; of course, the easy ones come first! Perhaps you sometimes laugh like someone else you know, or maybe you occasionally use a slang expression that a friend or work associate uses frequently. Often, whether or not your conscious mind likes the new behavior, the subconscious is already emulating your mentor.

We also have mentors in the business world. Certain professional organizations offer formal Mentor/Mentee programs, so that the newer people in a given profession can learn from those who have more experience and deserve emulation. A management trainee may look up to a professional mentor and start using the same "power phrases" and business jargon. The new employee may even hold a coffee cup the same way as the mentor (as I found myself doing when I became an insurance agent), consciously and subconsciously assuming that the path to success lies in totally imitating another successful person. In reality, the ego desires the praise and recognition that we believe the other person is receiving. Such emulation may evolve into something good, provided you choose your mentor wisely and exclude the bad traits—but beware! When the subconscious opens, what you do not monitor out may come in and stay!

Group Identification

Do you know someone who justifies an Irish temper? Perhaps an acquaintance looks down on you because you don't belong to the same church, political party, or race…

People tend to identify easily with groups: MY team, MY fraternity, MY country, etc. A special feeling comes along with belonging to a group or in identifying with a cause. The desire to belong seems closely related to peer pressure and appears to be universal. Some organizations often capitalize on this common desire to belong by encouraging members to surrender individual identity to a greater group identity! Such organizations frequently use this motivator to further the group goals, even to the detriment of the members. People with low self-images become especially vulnerable to this pressure.

Again, as with mentors, I consider group identification to be neither positive nor negative until so proven by individual results. Members make themselves vulnerable to subconscious programming that is based on group goals, methods, and the degree of individual involvement (as well as what the group member chooses to accept or reject). Many people belong to an organization, or a minority race, a church, etc., yet somehow learn to accept the good from the group and reject any negative input before it takes root in the subconscious. The risk of negative input grows with those who get so caught up in group causes that their minds become *completely closed* to other points of view.

Some years ago, people of my generation reeled in shock when Jim Jones motivated almost a thousand of his followers to commit suicide in South America. Many have wondered how that tragedy could possibly happen. Simply put, most members had such a strong desire to be part of this religious organization's group identity that *anything the group spokesman said went right into the subconscious*. This event will serve forever as an extreme example of group identification.

Religious cults often combine authority programming with peer pressure and group identity, doing a double whammy on the subconscious by speaking on God's behalf. Some cult leaders also employ group hypnosis, creating a *triple whammy*! Ministers of religious cults frequently use the phrase: "I didn't say this, God did!" Then, the personal opinions that follow go right into the subconscious minds of all those in the congregation who believe the first statement! The unfortunates who believed that Jim Jones spoke on God's behalf became tragic examples of this phenomenon.

I recommend that you make your own decisions rather than giving a representative of some organization carte blanche to program your mind as he/she chooses. If you have any remaining doubt about my advice, consider the shocking mass suicide of the Heaven's Gate cult. The cult members unknowingly allowed their leader to gain total access to their subconscious minds, giving him the ability to lead them to a tragic end.

Recognition

The "child inside" loves recognition and rewards as much as acceptance. Sales organizations bolster egos through programs that reward good sales performance. During my time in sales management, I found that some of my sales reps worked harder for a recognition award than for the monetary reward. Some people drive themselves to great heights for recognition in the business world, politics, sports, etc., often at great personal sacrifice. Many overinflated egos frequently don't care who gets stepped on, while others equally motivated by desire for recognition remain loving and likable. Somehow these considerate people learned how to use ego for personal motivation without becoming its slave, thus making ego a positive motivator and friend.

Alcoholics Anonymous also recognizes the motivation of good strokes. Some of my clients who quit drinking through the help of AA have indicated great pride in receiving their sobriety pins.

Often food serves as a reward. Clients seeing me for weight control frequently use food to recognize both their successes and failures—and then feel bad about it! Needless to say, their approach creates inner conflict.

I recommend that my clients choose the positive side of ego by planning both short-term and long-term rewards for themselves when working toward a goal. Whether or not we believe in rewards and recognition, these "warm fuzzies" influence us, so we might as well use them. Even the most negative person will sometimes do something to get attention, regardless of the benefits or consequences of that attention. Most of us still prefer "warm fuzzies" to cold criticism. Positive strokes tend to bring out the best in most of us, and genuine appreciation and positive recognition motivate us best of all.

Some people, unfortunately, never seem to learn the value of positive recognition. These negative critics continually tear other people down or find fault. Many parents harm their children's self-images (or self-identities) with statements such as: "You'll never amount to anything!" or "You can't do anything right." I urge parents to stop putting such negative programming into tomorrow's adults! Many people today seek therapy because of their own parents' negative criticism and abuse.

Employers, managers, and supervisors frequently fail to appreciate the importance of giving good strokes to employees. Some major businesses actually have unwritten codes against giving employees "outstanding" ratings on yearly reviews. *I STRONGLY disagree with this approach!* In my professional opinion, frequent employer criticism is dangerous to employee morale and loyalty. If an employee does an outstanding job, the employer should give both *praise* and a *raise*. Professional faultfinding takes its place as one more example of why so many people have self-esteem problems today. We live in a world where many people seem to be afraid to give another person a kind word. The critic would rather punch away at another's self-esteem, and then justify putting the other person down. Why can't we be willing to look for the good in others and compliment them?

We cannot control what others may or may not recognize in us, so I give clients the following three recommendations:

1. Don't give your power away by always depending on others to recognize you.
2. Learn to recognize your own strengths.
3. Celebrate your own successes and love yourself as much as your neighbor. (There's more about these rules in Chapter 10.)

God gave us ego. The inner child will seek recognition whether that attention comes in a positive or negative way. Unfortunately, trying to ignore our ego will not make it go away; but we can use ego positively while keeping a balance.

Left ignored, the ego can trip us up. By learning to use the energy of the ego in a positive way, however, we can enjoy a powerful ally for self-motivation. While exploring the good side of ego, let's learn to find positive things to say to others as well as to ourselves!

If you employ other people who help you earn your income, stroke their egos. Be sure to give the good employee *praise* and a *raise*!

Common *positive* ego motivators are desire for greater social acceptance (weight and smoking cessation), looking good (weight control), better self-image, pride of success or sense of accomplishment. Common *negative* ego motivators are: peer pressure (smokers), rewarding self (with food or cigs), resentment of social pressure, shame (because it causes us to fantasize the problem rather than the solution). Depending on your ego, you may have either a paved highway or a freeway passing through Gateway #3.

Gateway #4: Alpha (Hypnosis/self-hypnosis)

When your mind enters the alpha state, the subconscious becomes receptive to new programming.

As pointed out earlier, we can best describe hypnosis as guided self-hypnosis. Also remember that all hypnosis may also be called guided meditation, or *guided daydreaming*. Furthermore, *imagination is the language of the subconscious*; hypnosis facilitates one's ability to use imagination.

Remember that the subconscious responds to what we imagine, whether or not the input originates from an external source. For example, if the stage hypnotist suggests that you go to the North Pole and feel cold, you might be very distracted by focusing on how hot the stage lights make you feel. But if you imagine being in a blizzard, as suggested, your body might even produce goose bumps. You could just as easily get a desire to put on your coat by sitting in a movie theater watching a snow scene.

The person in hypnosis can imagine one hand in a bucket of ice and can actually feel the numbness. Better yet, the person in hypnosis can imagine achieving a goal, and the belief of possible achievement takes root in the subconscious. Sometimes you can control by yourself what you imagine. At other times, it's easier to allow someone or something else to guide you into creative imagination.

When you utilize a hypnotherapist or self-hypnosis tape, imagine the goals suggested to you rather than dwelling on the problems you wish to avoid. For example, if you listen to suggestions for weight control while imagining the taste of some goodies, your subconscious simply accepts what you imagine and you may find yourself wanting to eat when you emerge from hypnosis.

Increasing numbers of people around the country give testimony to the benefits of hypnosis for personal or business motivation. Many thousands of ex-smokers used hypnosis only as a last resort after exhausting others methods to kick the habit. People have learned how to control weight and eating habits through hypnotherapy. Sales people have enjoyed significant increases in income after only a few sessions. Others have improved at sports.

Among my clients are hundreds of former smokers who successfully quit. Numerous clients have reduced and kept the weight off. Former nail biters have long fingernails. A black belt immensely improved his timing in the martial arts. A swimmer won a silver medal in national competition. Some bowlers have improved their averages by more than a mark. Golfers have taken some strokes off their game. Sales people have doubled their incomes. One realtor turned his income into a six-digit figure. A hypnotherapist more than doubled the size of her practice. Just three months after her sessions, one salesperson ended the year at 245% of quota and within eighteen months became the branch manager. Shortly thereafter, she became a product manager for the entire company. When I last saw her, she had attained one of the company's top home-office executive positions. Hypnosis works.

Common *positive* hypnotic motivators are previous success with hypnosis (works at a subconscious level), hypnotherapy, and frequent use of self-hypnosis. Common *negative* hypnotic motivators are eating or smoking while watching TV, smoking in bed, midnight snacks, and frequent negative visualization of problems.

Entering the subconscious through the alpha gateway compares to driving on a superhighway (except that some highly analytical people sometimes create detours). While you may travel through that gate quickly, you still have the ability to steer provided you realize that YOU are the one in the driver's seat. Make certain that you take the right road.

Gateway #5: Emotion

Emotion is the motivating power of the mind. It compares to the *ace of trumps*, serving as the most powerful way possible to impact the subconscious. We don't walk through this gateway; we fly through it as though on a jet! Sometimes, however, we fly so fast that we miss important places along the way.

One minute of intense emotion can permanently impact the subconscious, as evidenced by one of my clients with a fear of water because she almost drowned during childhood. A former hypnotherapy student of mine spent over thirty years hating dogs because of a vicious attack during childhood. Another of my students spent most of his life fighting claustrophobia because his older brother trapped him inside a box for an hour and tormented him.

Whenever we enter an emotional state of mind, we become vulnerable to subconscious programming. Furthermore, as the emotions intensify, that emotional energy drives the imprints deeper into the subconscious. One doesn't have to be a psychologist to know that severe emotional traumas contribute to serious mental problems. It is dangerous to experience prolonged fear, sadness, or anger. If the emotions go to an extreme, the owners of these intense emotions could enter a state of deep depression and become totally unable to cope.

The results of intense emotional pain can take months or years of professional help to correct, such as with Viet Nam war veterans with posttraumatic stress syndrome who find themselves having flashbacks of the war. Such scars may require far more therapy than hypnosis alone can provide. How many people spend literally years of therapy dealing with the emotional aftermath of childhood traumas or past abuse? Many books have been written on this topic; widespread emotional trauma keeps the mental health profession quite busy. Stephen Parkhill, hypnotherapist and author, believes that cancer can usually be traced to intense negative emotions from which he has specialized in releasing people. Many of his clients have enjoyed profound improvements in their health!

Although I neither treat nor diagnose physical or mental illness, I recognize the importance of being careful about what we imagine whenever we experience emotion, especially because emotion serves as the most powerful of the five methods of subconscious programming.

Much has been said and written about the importance of controlling our emotions; I believe in going one step farther. We must monitor our thoughts when we experience any kind of emotion, whether that emotion is positive OR negative! For example, if you get frustrated at your boss or work associate and fantasize how you would like to respond, you may someday indeed find those same words jumping out of your mouth before you can stop them. When you rehearse certain words or actions mentally while experiencing emotion, your subconscious records these impressions. This rehearsal creates the potential for the imagined words or actions to come out automatically at a time or place you might regret, as numerous clients have already demonstrated before seeing me.

Does this mean we should never have feelings? I don't think so, because our emotions serve us! Our ability to feel emotion gives us wonderful abilities: to love, to enjoy, to appreciate the beauty of a sunset, to feel inspiration from beautiful music, to experience ecstasy with someone dearly loved, to know the contrasts between good times and sad times, or to *taste life*! Even the negative feelings help us appreciate the positive ones, as long as we remain in control. Controlling our emotions, however, means choosing *when* and *how* to express those feelings rather than simply stuffing them. In my opinion we must find a *balance*. Feel the feelings, express them, and then let them go. It is obvious that we should avoid loss of control during stress, but pretending to be calm and stuffing our emotions can be risky as well. For this reason, I encourage you to master the exercises for reducing stress (presented later in this book).

Emotion makes us even more vulnerable to suggestion than does hypnosis, so it behooves each of us to learn what to do when our buttons get pushed. Also, let's be aware that a positive emotion does not necessarily guarantee a positive result, nor does a negative emotion always produce a negative result.

For example, a new private, challenged by his drill sergeant in boot camp, could get angry and channel the energy into a desire to be a man and prove it! In my opinion, however, motivation by negative emotion can be dangerous in the business world. I knew a sales manager of a large corporation whose use of anger and fear motivation techniques backfired when a large percentage of his staff resigned in disgust. A veteran insurance professional with fifteen years of experience walked out of this manager's office one day, slamming the door behind her. She failed to produce to his satisfaction, so he "motivated" her by accusing her of being lazy and worthless. This insensitive man sprinkled his admonition with unprofessional language and threats, and spoke loudly enough for the rest of us to overhear. She resigned immediately, and then upper management asked for her former manager's resignation as well. The allegedly "lazy" woman became successful selling real estate.

Even today, some managers unwisely use fear and threats in order to increase employee productivity, and then wonder why they experience high employee turnover. One of my former Yellow Page representatives decided to quit in protest after his manager used fear tactics to try to motivate the sales staff. Management apparently threatened to fire anyone who didn't come within a few percentage points of the sales quota. Fear and anger sometimes motivate people to improve their work habits, but these methods often backfire and destroy employee morale.

Strangely enough, we can sometimes find some examples of negative results from positive feelings, evidenced partly by divorce courts. Also, we have all given into pleasurable emotions and overindulged in food, drink, or some other pleasure more times than we care to admit. On a more serious note, consider the fact that people who followed Jim Jones to their deaths originally found themselves drawn into his cult by warm emotional feelings of acceptance and perceptions of love. People who manipulate others frequently use love and positive emotions as well as guilt and fear.

We live in a manipulative world, with people constantly pushing our buttons. Whether the buttons push positive emotions or negative ones, WE must accept responsibility for choosing whether or not to buy into the manipulation. Loved ones often know exactly which buttons to push! Those who attempt to manipulate someone through guilt take a risk that may backfire. Many good relationships deteriorate quickly because of this dangerous game of manipulation through guilt: "If you really loved me, you'd..."

A positive emotion *usually* produces a positive result. Likewise, negative emotions normally create a greater risk of negative programming.

We tend to have a greater degree of control over the imagination while feeling positive feelings, but any emotion felt in the extreme opens us wide to sudden and lasting subconscious imprints and results in a very real need for us to control our emotions instead of allowing them to control us. Additionally, we need to be aware of what happens at a subconscious level when we experience emotions, so that we may monitor the input.

Common *positive* emotional motivators are loving the benefits and excitement at the realization of the goal itself. Common *negative* emotional motivators are guilt (damages the self-esteem) and using food or smoking to cope with stress. Also, people wishing to lose weight must contend with the (we wouldn't have it any other way) fact that food tastes good and gives us emotional satisfaction!

Summary

Lots of success techniques work, but unless the subconscious mind accepts the changes we desire, the old habits almost inevitably return. How do we gain that acceptance?

Repetition alone takes too long.

Authority is faster for some people but less effective for self-starters who often resent being told what to do. Furthermore, your own subconscious does not recognize you as an authority over yourself, one reason why we often rebel at attempts to use willpower. Remember that an immediate subconscious desire to obey or rebel serves as an example of how authority motivates the subconscious.

Desire for identity, used alone, has drawbacks, yet we can certainly supplement any plan by choosing a mentor wisely. Furthermore, we can gain improved self-esteem by learning to recognize our own successes.

Alpha (hypnosis) shines as the easiest of the five subconscious motivators.

Alpha increases your ability to consciously plan the proper road and monitor what takes place subconsciously. Even hypnosis, of and by itself, might not be sufficient to break old habit patterns.

Emotion is the motivating power of the mind and can propel you to success when used wisely. I highly recommend using self-hypnosis in combination with positive emotion for success. Realize, however, that people prone to the many emotional highs can also be subject to states of depression—negating positive programming. Most setbacks perpetuate themselves simply because of the emotional state of mind accompanying the setback. (When you imagine another failure while feeling emotion, you burn that failure deeper into your subconscious.)

Since emotion is the energy (or motivating power) of the mind, I recommend that we use hypnosis and/or self-hypnosis to learn to gain more control over our emotions, particularly the negative ones. Of course, we remain in control of our emotions more easily while feeling calm. This is logical. When feelings of anger, anxiety, or fear suddenly flood our awareness, however, we usually find difficulty staying in control without prior practice! While in the alpha state, we all have the ability to actually practice appropriate emotional responses in the rehearsal room of our imagination. Emotion plays such an important role in *making* or *breaking* our success that emotional control is vital.

The self-hypnosis exercises described in Chapter 8 will give you straightforward methods to help you take more control of your life and become less vulnerable to manipulation by others pushing your buttons. That chapter also discusses ownership and control of negative emotions as an important part of using a stress-coping technique. Many clients have told me that learning to manage stress with self-hypnosis ranks very high among the most valuable skills they have ever learned. Your emotions can serve you, or you can serve them. The choice is yours.

You'll find even more information concerning emotion in the chapter on creative daydreaming; for now let's look at how all the subconscious motivators can be utilized to motivate the subconscious to change a habit.

Chapter 7

The Quintuple Whammy

Now that you've read about the five gateways to the subconscious, let's consider their combined impact on the subconscious. I also call these motivators the methods of subconscious programming and have developed a unique approach to motivation.

It is obvious that the more any one motivator impacts the subconscious mind, the stronger the program becomes. The idea, belief, trigger, or "program tape" goes deep into the subconscious, but each gateway can allow both positive and negative input to enter, thereby causing inner conflicts. A strong desire to change a habit can be offset by subconscious resistance to change.

Let's consider the importance of recognizing all five subconscious gateways and of creating what I call a *motivation map*, or plan to use all five motivators to overcome the strength of the negative input working against us. I call this the *quintuple whammy*.

Hypnosis Alone Is Not Enough

Although self-hypnosis or hypnotherapy may be used to remove negative programming (as well as to enhance one's ability to regularly visualize the desired changes), hypnosis alone fails to outweigh certain kinds of subconscious negative motivators. If you've already tried hypnosis and failed to achieve your goal, this chapter may help you find additional means of effecting change.

Over the years, clients have often come to me saying that they had failed to respond to hypnotherapy. In some cases they had undergone hypnotic regression, etc., to help release the original cause of the habit. Then, even with a follow-up of positive suggestions, they wonder why they continue the bad habit. Negative input previously planted by an authority figure may indeed be removed by hypnotherapy, but other subconscious negative input often remains in place.

Also, many smokers have tried and failed with "thirty-minute" stop-smoking programs. Some programs advertise unbelievable success rates, which are *just that:* unbelievable and unprovable! One might think that such programs either would work for most people or not. Let's look at why people get drawn to these seminars.

In this fast-food society, people want something quick, cheap, and guaranteed—so many smoking-cessation programs "guarantee" success in only one session. In the Seattle area I've seen many of them advertising 97% success rates, when in reality four out of five participants smoke again within seven days. While 20% would be an acceptable success rate, advertising truthfully probably would not draw as many people. While these seminars work for some people, they do so only because more than one method of subconscious programming has already made the subconscious receptive to change. The hypnotist just makes enough difference to tip the scales toward success. (Some people who succeed in only one session never stop grieving for the loss of their *fair-weather friend*, and take up another addiction such as eating sweets.) Many who fail after trying these one-shot programs unfortunately and unnecessarily become skeptical of hypnosis.

Hypnosis remains very effective, but trance alone will never be a panacea for all of life's problems. Rather, we must use hypnosis in conjunction with other solutions.

Methods Working Against Desired Change

Now, to illustrate the combined use of all five motivators, let me recount the case history of a smoker who wanted to quit. It involves a process of information analysis that I call motivation mapping—a unique technique that I have taught to hypnotherapists on both coasts.

John (alias) had failed at ten prior attempts to quit smoking. Two attempts had involved hypnosis—one hotel seminar and one private session.

Repetition: He had years of practice of lighting up after certain triggers occurred (such as a ringing telephone). In the past he had tried to ignore those triggers, but the urges persisted, making it almost impossible for him to quit.

Authority: He started smoking to make a statement of rebellion against parental authority. He also resented his doctor telling him to quit.

Identity: John identified with smokers and resented increasing peer pressure to quit.

Alpha (hypnosis): John regularly smoked while watching TV, completely oblivious to the cigarettes until emptying his full ash tray after the eleven o'clock news. (TV induces hypnosis.)

Emotion: John always responded to stress buttons by "lighting up" to help him stuff his feelings.

Analysis: With this much subconscious programming working against John, he had virtually no way to change without using all five gateways positively.

Hypnotherapy could release him from the rebellion against old authority figures and could also enhance creative imagery for success. But John needed more. Furthermore, he had already failed at two previous hypnosis programs. The quickie, one-session hotel seminar increased his belief that he would get a major disease, yet that fear failed to make him quit. His one private hypnotherapy session incorporated only posthypnotic suggestion to avoid smoking but failed to help him replace his fair-weather friend. John's motivation map indicated that he would have to use a quintuple whammy in order to quit smoking for good!

Combining the Programming Methods

I helped John combine all five programming methods. Since his case is similar to many, my quintuple whammy recommendations have broad application.

Repetition: I suggested that he get into the habit of taking one deep breath of air whenever one of the old smoking triggers occurred. (Refer to the section on Anchoring and Triggers at the end of Chapter 5.) One deep breath has no calories and can be taken anywhere!

Remember that we can often *replace* a habitual conditioned response (light up) with another conditioned response (deep breath), but trying to erase that habit can prove to be far more difficult. It is also important to replace the old response with one that is harmless and not, for example, to replace smoking with snacking.

Authority: John recognized the medical authority of proven health statistics. Health was his primary motive for quitting, so authority was already part of his positive motivation. Nevertheless, he continued to resist his personal physician's advice to quit.

The subconscious tends to rebel against force. Rebellion is—in a simplistic form—resistance against manipulation regardless of the consequences. John resented others trying to manipulate him into quitting, but in reality he allowed the actions of others to *manipulate* him *into smoking*! He had decided to exercise his power of choice, regardless of the consequences. He could now use the same power to rebel against the cigarette. Furthermore, John believed in God and decided to use prayer power to obtain help from the highest authority.

Desire for identity: John decided to enjoy the sense of accomplishment obtained from successfully quitting. He allowed this sense of accomplishment to become part of his new identity as a totally tolerant nonsmoker. To help him with this new identity, I suggested that he reward his successes with the money that used to go up in smoke. We established his reward intervals at one week, one month, three months, and one year.

Alpha: To help John become less vulnerable to the hypnotic influence of television, I recommended that he replace TV smoking with water or another noncaloric beverage of his choice. I also gave him a self-hypnosis antismoking tape designed to help him imagine his desired success.

Emotion: To help minimize stress, I taught John the stress-coping technique described in the next chapter of this book. I also had him imagine his personal benefits and bond emotionally with them.

Combining the Motivators for Weight Management

I usually recommend that people who want to stop overeating use a quintuple whammy.

Emotion benefits us when we fantasize the benefits of being at an ideal weight. To offset the emotional bond to food, you must create some emotional desire to succeed. If your weight makes you feel guilty, *forgive* yourself! The fastest way to release guilt is through forgiveness. The preceding chapters should have helped you realize that the deck might be stacked against you; you have no reason to hang on to any guilt. Enjoy the sense of satisfaction that comes from looking and feeling good. Allow yourself to fall in love with the benefits!

Alpha (hypnosis) is more effective when it is combined with the other motivators.

People who require only minimal motivation may find sufficient help by mastering the self-hypnosis exercises in this book. Remember that TV induces trance, so avoid snacking while watching television. If needed, replace the snacks with water or a low-cal beverage. When strong subconscious resistance exists, however, a combination of group or private hypnotherapy sessions and a self-hypnosis tape may be necessary. In most cases, however, weight reduction requires the quintuple whammy for long-term success.

Desire for identity is a motivator that enables the ego to serve us rather than vice versa. Find a mentor. Admire someone who does well at controlling his/her weight, and then emulate your mentor's strengths. Also, reward yourself for your successes along the way (every five pounds, etc.) and make certain that you remember to *celebrate your successes*. When you succeed at motivating yourself to change a habit, the little child inside will strongly desire attention and recognition. If you have difficulty creating a positive identity, then you may need to work on self-esteem (covered in a later chapter).

Authority is important, because you need a proven plan that really works. Some fad diets are dangerous, and many so-called authorities stretch the truth about their knowledge of nutrition. Belief in God also opens up the subconscious in certain situations. If you believe in a higher power, pray for help. If you have a healthy "rebel" button, use it as an ally to rebel against junk food.

Repetition of any and all of the above programming methods reinforces their impact on the subconscious. If you are a member of the clean-plate club, get into the habit of leaving a little food on your plate. If you eat too fast, frequently remind yourself to *eat slowly!*

Using all five gateways into the subconscious remains almost essential in long-term weight control because of the strength of past programming and the continual bombardment from society to activate old, subconscious tapes.

What About Other Goals?

For goals other than weight control or quitting smoking, this process can often be easier because the forces working against you may not be as severe, as shown by a number of motivation maps I have developed for individuals. Yet some people have old habits and thought patterns that may be even harder to change than smoking or overeating, especially if energized with negative emotion during unpleasant experiences.

One of my goals is to teach my clients to *be aware of what is imagined* whenever the subconscious mind opens up. Understanding the five gateways to the subconscious (or subconscious motivators) is essential to such awareness. With this understanding, you can maintain greater control of the changes you choose to make in your life.

Later chapters in this book discuss setting goals and establishing priorities, and describe numerous empowerment exercises to help you achieve your goals. Once you have done these exercises, you may wish to refer to this and the preceding chapter for help identifying sources of negative subconscious input and starting to monitor them carefully. Next, you can look for ways to use as many of the five subconscious motivators as possible to give yourself positive input, thereby improving your chances for success.

Now let's explore some empowerment exercises to help manage stress.

Chapter 8

Exercises to Manage Stress

This chapter contains three self-hypnosis empowerment exercises designed to help with three different phases of stress: coping at the moment stress occurs, calming down after stress with a mental mini-vacation, and sleeping at night (rather than worrying) during times of stress.

Let's start by considering our options when things seem fine…until somebody pushes the wrong buttons.

What to Do When Your Buttons Get Pushed

Many outstanding professionals provide excellent advice to help you reduce stress both at work and at home, and many books and seminars offer help with stress management. But what do you do when someone still happens to push your buttons? As long as we have the "three T's" (teenagers, traffic jams, and telephones), our buttons will get pushed. In other words, it's not a question of whether our buttons will get pushed, it's only a question of where and when … and then what?

The first empowerment exercise helps you create a simple coping technique to help you during emotional anxiety.

Since emotion is such a powerful door to the subconscious, I teach the importance of learning how to control emotions by making a positive choice at the time our buttons get pushed. (The healthy choices follow the directions for the exercise in this chapter.) We must also accept ownership of our emotions (even negative ones). So if you tell yourself: *Xxxx made me mad,* you just gave your power away. Rather, you should realize that Xxxx sold you some stress, and you *bought* it—and now *you* own it, and you have the power of choice to decide what to do with the stressful emotion!

Let me draw from my experience as a parent of teenagers to illustrate further. When a member of the younger generation has a temper tantrum, I *just might occasionally* buy into some anger! As they grow up, some children learn to be quite effective at selling stress. Reaching the *teens* somehow seems to enhance their skill at selling negativity, but sometimes I refuse to buy into their negative emotions. In simple terms, while I cannot control the actions of a teenager, I (and I *alone*) must accept responsibility for *my* responses to the teenager's actions! My children have certainly provided me with sufficient opportunities to walk my talk! (Often it seems that those we love the most are best able to push our buttons.)

Several years ago a public opportunity for me to walk my talk presented itself in front of a hundred of my peers. Just minutes into my presentation on *stress management,* the table on the stage came crashing down with a thud! The pitcher and two glasses went flying, breaking into scores of pieces beside me. Water and ice spread quickly at my feet, mingled with broken glass. Thinking quickly on my feet, I said, *Well, I didn't know this would be experiential!* Then the microphone made a loud, high-pitched sound. I took one deep breath and exclaimed, *Thank you, God!* After my presentation concluded, several participants asked me how I could plan a demonstration to look so authentic!

Now, let's get on with the instructions for the first stress-management exercise.

To maximize the benefits of the stress-coping technique, you must practice the coping skill several times in the rehearsal room of your imagination while in a state of self-hypnosis. Practicing at a quiet time when your emotions remain calm helps your subconscious mind accept the desired technique. The exercise is a rehearsal, which any performer knows is essential to a good performance.

When you are ready to begin, get relaxed and comfortable, as suggested in the first practice session. Read and understand the instructions before proceeding, so that you don't have to refer to them once you begin. (If you have not already done so, practice the simple self-hypnosis inductions given in Chapter 3 until you succeed with at least one induction method. Also remember to remove hard contact lenses and get rid of any chewing gum.)

Next, read the affirmations on stress management at the end of this book. Read them slowly and deliberately—either silently or out loud.

Now you may enter self-hypnosis through the method I described in the first practice session. Daydream yourself into a totally peaceful place. Imagine pleasant and peaceful sights, sounds, and/or feelings. As you do, take a deep breath and think the word *relax* as you exhale. (Some readers first may need to master the "mental mini-vacation" exercise described later in this chapter.)

Daydream your ability to remain calm in a scenario you rehearse in your mind where someone tries to push your buttons. Physically take the deep breath—thinking the word *relax* as you exhale. Imagine your ability to actually feel calm, confident, and composed—totally in control of your feelings. Fantasize making one of the three choices described under "Stress Release Options" below. Imagine yourself feeling calm, confident, and in control of your emotions. Imagine the situation through to a desirable conclusion. Practice the other two choices in the same manner.

When you are ready, come back to the beta state by counting from one to five.

Stress Release Options: the Healthy Choices

We may choose from among three healthy options when our buttons get pushed:

1. Express yourself immediately but appropriately

Some situations, such as when your child does something dangerous or a customer raises an objection during a "closing interview", require an immediate response. You may find emotion reflected in your voice in the first example, and you may have to wait until you've yelled "NO!!!" before taking your deep breath. In the second example, you may wish to take a deep breath first, then simply express yourself calmly and confidently. In some situations, you may wish to find the humorous side of the situation. Laughter can be a good release; sometimes, tears; sometimes, one word spoken firmly; sometimes sarcasm; etc.

2. Express yourself later at a more appropriate time and place

This option might be in your best interest if an associate at work pushes the wrong button in the presence of others. Some people will accept your opinion much more readily in private over coffee or tea rather than in front of peers. Furthermore, parents frequently find meals more enjoyable by instructing their children to wait until after dinner to resolve their arguments.

3. Release and let go—or forgive!

If you don't choose either of the first two options, then practice this one (you do not have to condone). If you think someone else owes you an apology, you place yourself in bondage to that belief. By freeing others from their emotional debts, you actually free yourself. The key to forgiving involves the ability to release the other person from the apology formerly owed, and to *also forgive yourself* for buying the stress in the first place. Release might be the wisest option if your boss pushes your buttons.

Most people use other options, such as stuffing or internalizing bad feelings, for stress control, with varying consequences. We might take our stress out on friends or loved ones. We could take it out on strangers. We might also take it out on the same person at a later date through blowing up something out of all proportion. Worse yet, some people take it out on themselves through sickness, escapism, addiction, or by becoming accident-prone. Some people react to stress with an uncontrolled, immediate, emotional expression. All these options are hazardous to your health and wealth!

In going through the healthy scenarios during self-hypnosis, remember to rehearse each of the three healthy choices. Your rehearsal during self-hypnosis influences your performance during real-life stress, like posthypnotic suggestions. You will now allow your subconscious to respond to a given signal, and *you decide when to give the signal*. Practicing during the trance state anchors the power of choice into your signal, creating a trigger for choice! As an added benefit, your trigger for choice becomes a form of empowerment at a subconscious level.

This simple technique alone can improve family relationships and social relationships. In any discussion where opinions might differ, emotion can transfer from one person's subconscious to another's, compounding the anxiety of all parties concerned. Confidence can also transfer from subconscious to subconscious, increasing the probability of peaceful resolution.

Business people may discover that mastering these three responses increases their income! If someone in a sales interview fears losing a sale after an unexpected objection, the prospective customer may subconsciously pick up on that fear. While the sales rep might fear losing the sale, the prospect fears making a decision—and will want to *think it over* instead of giving you the real objection. Confidence also comes across at a subconscious level, making the customer more prone to either buy confidently or reveal the real objection.

Using the Coping Technique

The deep breath becomes your trigger for choice: *now, later,* or *release.* The deep-breath trigger becomes a reminder to you that you own your own emotions, and *you* have the *power of choice!*

Understand, too, that your degree of success in coping may vary according to the situation at hand—as well as the frequency with which you use your new technique. Exercising a muscle creates strength, so you could think to yourself: *As a muscle that's used becomes stronger with use, my power of choice becomes stronger with use!*

After you complete this practice session, notice opportunities to practice your new skill. Next time you drive and someone turns left in front of you, take a deep breath and think the word *relax.* If you feel like calling him a jerk first, go ahead—as long as you still take the deep breath before or afterward.

The workplace is another great place to practice this skill. Suppose you want to go home after a hectic day on the job, but suddenly find out you have to stay late because someone else didn't finish a job. Take one deep breath, think *relax,* and then say and do what seems most appropriate. Many of my clients have reported to me an improvement in their own self-confidence simply from mastering the art of this technique.

Let's suppose you have a day riddled with stress. You have a few moments alone in your office, or you've already come home feeling overloaded with the day's stresses. This might be the time to take a mental mini-vacation!

The Mental Mini-Vacation

Your imagination is a rehearsal room where you have the ability to practice being the person you wish to be! You can imagine what you plan on doing tomorrow, or you can replay what happened yesterday.

Quite frequently we use imagination to anticipate the pleasure of a planned long weekend—when we finally get out to the lake, on the golf course, to the campground or the beach, etc. Dating couples can attest to the fact that anticipation influences both the mind and body! I'll avoid describing what frequently takes place in the imagination during a date, yet I'll remind the reader that both the mind and body will respond to the imagination! Both mind and body respond just as easily to fantasized places of peace and beauty.

Consider your imagination to be your own private place, where you can travel through time and space. *Star Trek* viewers can compare the imagination to the *holodeck of the mind,* because you can create your own program! In your imagination you can BE anywhere you wish, and DO anything you wish.... You can relive any memory (happy or sad), or you can experience any fantasy. Although many of our parents taught us not to daydream, we can't avoid daydreaming occasionally. The question is whether you control your daydreams, or vice versa.

The mental mini-vacation utilizes your ability to daydream. You may enjoy going back in time to a favorite vacation spot, or you may imagine going forward in time to a future vacation. You have the choice! Remember that you have total power, total freedom, and total privacy in your imagination. You can do anything you wish, and go anywhere you wish. Are you ready?

Enter self-hypnosis using your chosen induction, then adapt the following script to your own words. Again, notice that the simple wording means more to the subconscious than good grammar...

I'm going to count backward now from ten to one. As I do, it becomes easier and easier for me to imagine sights, sounds and feelings in my beautiful, peaceful place...

Number ten—deeper and deeper, relaxing physically... With each breath, it's easier to imagine my peaceful place...

Number nine—deeper and deeper, relaxing mentally... With each sound, it's easier to imagine pleasant sights, sounds, and feelings...

Number eight—deeper and deeper, relaxing emotionally... The deeper I go, the better I feel, and the deeper I want to go...

Number seven—deeper and deeper, relaxing totally... The deeper I go, the easier it is to go even deeper, imagining my peaceful place...

Number six—every nerve and muscle relaxes completely... as if I'm becoming a part of the peace that I imagine...

Number five—each number making it easier and easier to go deeper and deeper... and it feels SO good to just relax...

Number four—as I go deeper, it becomes easier and easier to imagine sights, sounds, and feelings that are so calm, and so peaceful...

Number three—just drifting into total relaxation... into my place of total peace... where I can enjoy being anywhere I wish now...

Number two—just relaxing at my ideal peaceful place now...

Number one—waaaaaaaaaaaaaay down deep... Relaxing into a very deep, inner peace... a very deep, inner peace...

As I touch my finger to my thumb, or take a deep breath and think the word RELAX, it's an automatic reminder of my inner peace. [Touch a finger to your thumb, and take a deep breath.] Whenever I do this in the waking state, I feel calm and composed, free to think with a clear mind... but for now, I can just enjoy going even deeper into relaxation... deeper and deeper...

With each breath I take, it's easier and easier to enjoy my freedom of imagination, to go to a favorite vacation spot now... and imagine my IDEAL vacation... doing what I enjoy doing, and relaxing as well...

In my mind, as much time as I wish can pass... and I feel as though I've enjoyed an hour's nap... I feel like I enjoyed an hour's nap...

Before emerging from trance, imagine feeling the way you wish to feel! Then, when ready, count forward from one to five and awaken yourself.

Most hypnotherapists use a method like this one to help clients establish a peaceful place. The act of taking the deep breath (or touching your thumb and finger) WHILE imagining your peaceful place anchors a sense of inner peace to that act. Anchoring your peaceful place into your trigger during trance compares to programming your computer. Activating your trigger during the conscious state compares to pushing the "Execute" button on your computer. Your deep breath (and/or touching thumb and finger) will now become a trigger for *inner peace!*

Use your *inner peace* trigger in conjunction with your stress-coping technique, and notice an increased ability to cope with life's stresses. (You can also call this the *peaceful place trigger.*)

Sleeping at Night

Have you ever found yourself unable to sleep easily because of stress or worry? If you can honestly answer NO to that question, count your blessings and skip down to the next chapter; otherwise, keep on reading.

Frequently I've used self-hypnosis to go to sleep easily at night, and I have taught clients to do likewise. Most of the time the mental mini-vacation technique adequately helps people fall asleep even during stressful times; sometimes a major stress can inhibit one's ability to respond to the techniques described thus far in this book. For the benefit of readers experiencing the same difficulty, here is another technique that may work wonders. This unusual self-hypnosis exercise consistently proves valuable for me personally—and for clients as well.

FIRST, be aware that some sleeping disorders may have physical causes; please consult with your physician if you have any reason whatsoever to believe that more than just stress keeps you awake. Also, if your stress seems related to serious unresolved emotional issues and/or family problems, consider seeking the help of a competent professional. (For your own protection, similar advice appears several times throughout this book, as repetition is good emphasis.) Anyone on medication because of insomnia may also need to consult with a physician prior to using this next exercise. Now that I've given my words of caution, let's continue.

One main type of trance induction employs what hypnotherapists call *mental confusion*. Mental exercises that cause the logical mind to sort through confusing input can also create a trance state! Many hypnotherapists guide their clients into trance with mental-confusion techniques; I've adapted one to be a simple self-hypnosis technique for going to sleep. Causing the conscious to work at a time when we prefer to rest will allow some interesting things to happen at a subconscious level.

Remember when your parents told you to count sheep at night in order to fall asleep? Adding a few autosuggestions to that same child's technique can produce an alpha state that soon turns into theta and delta ... resulting in sound sleep. My variation involves counting backward rather than forward, and you may imagine the numbers any way you wish. These numbers may appear on sheep (or other animals) passing by, jumping over a fence, etc.; or the numbers may be on signposts (or any other visual image) or simply whispered by the wind.

When you notice that your mind wants to wander away from the technique, you should be closer to drifting off to sleep. What you say to yourself at this point can *help or hinder*, so learn from my experience. First, find a comfortable position and then take three very deep breaths. Continue breathing slowly and deeply. Say to yourself words similar to those in the following script...

> As I count backward from 100, one number per breath, my mind just wishes to drift off to sleep... 100. [Inhale.]
>
> I can imagine seeing or hearing each number just before I say it to myself... 99. [Inhale.]
>
> As I imagine my peaceful place, with pleasant sights, sounds, and feelings, the numbers start getting farther away... 98. [Inhale.]
>
> As the numbers get smaller and smaller, I get sleepier and sleepier, wanting to wander asleep... 97. [Inhale.]

My mind starts wandering as I wander closer to the realm of deep sleep, getting sleepy… 96. [Inhale.]

The more my mind wanders, the sleepier I get… and my mind wanders away from remembering the numbers… 95. [Inhale.]

The numbers get easier to forget, or difficult to remember, and I get sleepier and sleepier… 94. [Inhale.]

When I forget the last number, or skip the next number, or repeat a number, it DOUBLES my drowsiness… [Next #; inhale.]

If I take two breaths between numbers, or remember to forget, or forget to remember, my mind just wants to sleep… [Next #; inhale.]

The more I try to remember to forget, or skip or repeat, the last number or the next one, the sleepier I get… [Next #; inhale.]

As it becomes easier to fantasize my peaceful place, I soon find myself dreaming of my peaceful place… [Next #; inhale.]

The numbers are getting farther and farther, smaller and smaller, deeper and deeper, into sleep… [Next #; inhale.]

I TRY to stay with the numbers, but my mind wants to wander… or drift… and wander… to sleep… [Next #; inhale.]

As I skip numbers, repeat numbers, or forget numbers, I go deeper and deeper into sleep… [Next #; inhale.]

If you are still awake at this point, take two breaths between numbers and imagine that the numbers (or sheep) gradually move farther and farther away.

Now I take two breaths between each number, and it gives my mind more time to wander to sleep… [Inhale.]

The more I try to remember the script, the easier it is for my mind to wander, or the sleepier I get… [Next #; inhale.]

If I think of two numbers in a breath, or breathe three times between numbers, I get MUCH sleepier… [Inhale.]

It would be SO much easier to simply forget about the numbers and just let myself go to sleep… [Next #; inhale.]

As I try to remember to forget the numbers or the script, my mind simply finds it easier to doze off, or sleep… [Inhale.]

As the numbers start jumping around now, I get sleepier and sleepier, or drowsy and sleepy… [Next #; inhale.]

I don't know if I forgot the last number, or the next number, or both, because my mind wanders more… [Inhale.]

It's SO much easier to simply imagine a pleasant place, until what I imagine becomes a dream… [Inhale.]

The numbers are fading farther away, allowing my mind to wander and dream… or dream and wander… [Inhale.]

If you still find yourself awake, simply continue counting backward while whispering words similar to those contained in the script. Be sure your breathing remains slow and easy. Most people using this technique properly will rarely get clear down to the last number before falling asleep, although I've been an exception twice in ten years. On one of those occasions, I remember whispering to God, *Well, God, I got clear down to Number One. It didn't work this time* … and that was the last thing I remembered before waking up the next morning!

Other People's Successes

How effective are these empowerment exercises? I can best answer that question by providing a summary of satisfied-client case...

Roger (alias) devoted himself to his family, his church, and his career. In spite of unexpected financial setbacks and professional frustrations, he continued to put forth quality work for his employer. Within a few short months, he found himself in such an emotional mess that he worked more hours weekly to accomplish less than when he worked normal hours. The cycle of stress resulted in lost sleep, increasing anxieties, and marital problems. While I could not advise him regarding the marital stress, he strongly desired to learn how to simply respond more maturely whenever somebody pushed his buttons. Although he originally saw me for habit control, he told me that the benefits derived from learning the stress-coping technique proved to be worth the investment in an entire series of sessions. The stress coper enabled him to pause just long enough to make better responses, thus increasing his sense of empowerment as well as building his self-esteem.

The majority of clients practicing stress management meditation have reported benefits over the years, ranging from slight to profound. The degree of help depends on both the need and the commitment of the person utilizing this technique.

Many clients have thanked me for teaching the peaceful-place meditation, or the mental mini-vacation. Often just ten minutes in a self-hypnotic trance can provide as much benefit as a one-hour nap.

While the sleep exercise benefits many clients, I find one fact quite interesting: very few clients have ever seen me for insomnia. The majority who have seen me for sleeping disorders (nonmedical) have often encountered subconscious resistance. On the other hand, hundreds of clients over the years seeing me for habit control have reported sleeping *better than in years* simply after mastering the art of self-hypnosis.

Master at least one of the above empowerment exercises to help you manage stress. In my opinion, you will be glad you did. Then, when you feel ready to learn more, go right on to the next part of my book and prepare your journey toward successful goal achievement.

Part Three

Planning the Journey

Chapter 9

Clearing Obstacles

Now that we have seen how we can program the subconscious, let's consider life's journey itself. We cannot reach a chosen destination without choosing the right road or path, and we must also clear away any obstacles or find a way around them. How do we clear the obstacles? How do we find the best path toward our goals? This chapter answers the first question; the next three chapters will answer the second question.

Obstacles and negative thinking seem to attract each other, so take a look inward at any habits or repetitive, negative thought patterns you may wish to change. You may recognize the influence of some subconscious programming. For example, most smokers started because of the desire to identify with peers or adults, but often feel a desire to light up whenever someone tells them to quit. Overeating sometimes relates to low self-esteem, which often can be traced either to past failures and/or to negative emotional experiences. As a general rule, we need to *release the past* before we can change negative thinking and clear the obstacles.

The consequences of hanging on to the past could compound themselves, creating bigger obstacles and trapping us into negative thinking. This chapter explains why, discusses some common traps caused by various failures and hurts, and shows how to release them. Notice how some traps overlap others.

The Failure Trap

Have you ever felt trapped by a series of relentless failures and setbacks?

We attract what we imagine—the reason why failure often attracts more failure. Indulging in self-pity creates an accompanying negative emotion, opening wide the subconscious gateways. The danger occurs when we relive failures in the imagination and continuously replay them. The more you imagine failure, the more likely your chances of failing again. This principle applies whether your goal involves sports, business, or simply overcoming an undesired habit. The cycle is likely to continue until both the imagination and the feelings change!

During a slump, an athlete often finds negative feelings compounding in a manner that sends him/her into a downward spiral of doubt. If the athlete believes in the slump and replays recent failures, the subconscious receives negative suggestions through the language of imagination. Normally the cycle will continue until it is broken by a good performance.

For a salesperson experiencing a self-perpetuating sales slump, it becomes all too easy to imagine the dreaded objection. Fantasizing customer objections will actually influence the subconscious to construct a negative presentation. The emotion and slump may change with a big sale, but that big sale normally requires imagining the desired success first.

The smoker who feels guilty for always backsliding often puts energy into the fear of lighting up. Replaying past failures sends a message to the inner mind, attracting yet another failure.

The frequent dieter often remembers indulging in goodies and blowing past diets; if he/she believes that another diet will fail, guess what happens!

Even when we consciously want to overcome failure, the acceptance of past failures tends to attract more failure because we keep imagining it. Trying to use logic alone to overcome a painful setback can be ineffective, because negative daydreaming leads to justification of failure. We must break this cycle by training ourselves to imagine success, to replace a negative fantasy with a positive one. We will lose in the land of logic, so we must win in the field of daydreams! When we are ready to analyze a failure, we must keep our emotions in check and avoid replaying the failures lest we fall victim to the justification trap.

The Justification Trap

Have you found yourself among those who are so involved with analyzing the reasons for failure that you find the success you seek slipping farther away? As long as you search for reasons to justify your failure, you will continue to fail.

Our society invests considerable time, money, and effort studying reasons for failure. Hindsight may bring insight but, to find success, we need to invest the majority of our time and energy in *where we are going* instead of where we have been. By spending your energy searching for roadblocks, your subconscious mind may very well be creating new obstacles, keeping you locked inside the *justification trap*.

I know people who have spent years going to counselors or hypnotherapists to look for CAUSES of problems, only to end up finding more real or imagined roadblocks from the past to justify holding on to their problems. Some search the past diligently for reasons to blame a third party for negative programming. Unless we explore the past with the intention of *releasing* it and learning from our mistakes, we risk falling into the *self-pity pit*.

Wallowing around in self-pity and/or prolonged anger over past hurts usually leads to further justification of failure by blaming others, thus creating greater difficulty in our efforts to change negative feelings. The self-pity pit permits more failure because our behavior now becomes easier to justify, and our obstacles appear bigger.

Another trap often accompanying the self-pity pit is the "If only" trap.

"If Only..."

This commonly heard phrase haunts many of us. Can you think of times where a goal might have been realized if only circumstances had been just a little different?

A smoker says, *If only my friend hadn't pushed my buttons...*

A dieter says, *If only my spouse hadn't eaten dessert in front of me...*

A salesperson says, *If only the competition had called one day later...*

A student says, *If only I had one more day to study...*

An athlete says, *If only the umpire hadn't made that bad call…*

"If only" makes it easy to continue justifying a problem by its apparent cause(s). We can easily defeat ourselves by getting emotionally involved with reasons for failure. I know, because I've been there. When "if only" becomes a habit, we can start feeling like we are a victim in a trap—success will have a way of eluding us until we get out of it. Taken to an extreme, some people might engage in antisocial behavior by saying, "If only I hadn't been abused, I could live a normal life," because it's easier to blame others for their unacceptable behavior than to accept responsibility for their actions.

Do you engage in "if only" thinking? If so, perhaps it's time to forgive those who have hurt you so that you can get on with life.

Forgiveness and Responsibility

I often tell my hypnotherapy students that there is no magic in hypnosis, but there is often magic in forgiveness. This point is often the most controversial one in my entire nine-month hypnotherapy course.

It is human nature to hold on to anger against those who have hurt us until they pay for their mistakes. Forgiving others does not mean condoning their actions or requiring you to forget how they might have hurt you, but it does mean that you have to "let go" of your anger toward them for those past hurts. Why? Because forgiveness provides a powerful key to escaping the traps described above. We might wisely choose to separate ourselves from a bad situation for our own protection (or to put a criminal behind bars for the protection of society), but we must escape from our own grudges in order to be free.

I believe that we are the ones who remain in bondage to grudges … not the people who hurt us. Until we learn to let go of anger over past hurts, it may be virtually impossible to clear the obstacles in our path and make the changes we desire. Some experts seem to prefer that their clients keep their anger and stay in counseling for years, taking your money and helping you discover all kinds of causes for your problems. These alleged causes might tempt you to put more energy into keeping your problems in the belief that you might be more "functional" today IF ONLY someone else had not been responsible for harming or abusing you. Some counselors claim that we can regain our power only by confronting the perpetrator! In my view, forgiveness outshines blame and is absolutely essential for complete healing. At the very least, we must release the other person to his/her higher power (or karmic fate) and forgive ourselves for carrying the hurt.

One of my clients (in her forties) told me that another counselor, as a condition of healing, instructed her to confront her father for alleged childhood abuse! If this happens to you, you might benefit by looking for another therapist. You don't need to hear someone say that you'd be normal "if only" you had not been abused.

I have experienced the healing power of forgiving the abuse I received from a cousin during childhood. Forgiving and releasing resulted in my ability to heal and get on with life and, contrary to the opinion of a psychotherapist, I am NOT scarred for life. My choice was either to heal through forgiveness or to say, *If only he hadn't hurt me, I could be normal.* I'm grateful that I chose the path of forgiveness.

Regardless of our past, we can change our present response to it. Don't stay in the victim trap. Regardless of what pain and stress others might inflict upon us, we must all accept responsibility for our reactions to other people, places, and things. (If you currently feel trapped in stressful family problems and/or a bad job, etc., seek competent professional help from an appropriate source.)

At the opposite extreme, we find people whose idea of "accepting responsibility" means that YOU are somehow responsible for the actions of people who hurt you. Accepting your own responsibility does not mean accepting responsibility for the actions of others—but rather only for your own actions! You need to find the balance between the two. When you determine what your share of the responsibility is, learn from it and forgive yourself also, because forgiving yourself is equally as important as forgiving others.

Dealing with Criticism

Unexpected criticism often challenges our ability to forgive ourselves and others. Without commenting about handling the particulars of any specific criticism, I must address the importance of the subconscious reaction we have to a negative putdown or character slam. How we handle the criticism determines whether we will remove obstacles or build more obstacles. It would be easy to write an entire book about how to give and receive criticism, but I'll only make a few important comments here.

Our response might be influenced by the combination of our own attitude at the time, the attitude and motives of the critic, the relevancy of the criticism, and whether or not we asked for it. Additionally, we might expect constructive criticism from an employer or supervisor, but a variety of factors may influence its impact on the subconscious. We might not be as willing to receive criticism from a friend, unless it is given constructively with a motive to help.

During a convention in 1997, Peter J. Daniels, a very successful Australian businessman, gave an interesting presentation on dealing with negative criticism. He said that negative criticism binds the receiver while giving a sense of power to the sender, and he encouraged us to avoid buying into negative criticism.

Many of us have experienced less-than-satisfying encounters with self-appointed teachers who try to convince us to accept responsibility for "creating the reality" of attracting manipulators or abusers into our lives. I have concluded that some people would rather blame someone else for "creating a poverty consciousness" as an excuse to justify their own greed; I have known people who, under the guise of spirituality, take unfair advantage of others' time and talents in self-serving ways. Then, when the victim tries to assert himself/herself, the user lectures the victim about accepting responsibility and/or "manifesting a prosperity consciousness." When you recognize such greed, you would be wise to remove yourself. You can forgive the user, but you do NOT have to allow him to convince you that you are the one with the problem.

We can be responsible only for how we respond to others. Sometimes the best response is to physically separate ourselves from someone who hurts us repeatedly or tries to take advantage of us. Give your time and talents to people who recognize you and appreciate you. Success comes more easily to those who are free of incessant criticism. Just maintain enough internal integrity to determine whether or not there is any validity to the criticism, regardless of the motive and manner of the sender. If in doubt, seek counsel from a trusted friend or professional.

What if the criticism you receive is valid?

Self-criticism

Upon recognizing truth in a criticism, look for solutions rather than putting energy into the problem. If your critic genuinely wants to help, ask him/her to suggest solutions. If he/she tried to hurt you, but gave a valid criticism, then look elsewhere. Don't come down too hard on yourself, since indulging in excessive self-criticism can send you right back into the self-pity pit. Many people don't realize that success does not mean doing things perfectly, nor does it mean having a fat bank account. People often criticize themselves for not having enough money and/or for being less than perfect. If we wait until we find perfection, success may elude us.

A semipro bowler, who was seeing me for sports improvement, demonstrated the power that even minor self-criticism can have when accompanied with negative emotions, thereby energizing the *problem* rather than the solution. He said, "Whenever I leave the 10-pin by itself, I always get nervous and blow the spare." His self-criticism worsened the problem and reinforced the failure he imagined every time he left the 10-pin standing. After some private sessions to help him focus on the desired result instead of the problem, his self-criticism stopped and his average improved by seventeen pins.

Indulging in self-criticism creates guilt, destroys motivation, and compounds problems. Many people literally stress themselves into illness through constant self-criticism. Looking for better ways of doing things can be constructive if done without putting yourself down; throwing mud at yourself for mistakes or financial setbacks only damages your self-esteem. While a brief moment of guilt might induce us to change our actions or minimize antisocial behavior, indulging in prolonged guilt can cripple us and be hazardous to our health and wealth. We need to learn from our mistakes, and those of others, then RELEASE the mistakes and *get on with life!*

Techniques for Releasing

So how do we release? A person with a painful past may need far more help than I can provide here, but let me begin by offering some techniques that might help with past hurts, and then deal with some for present hurts.

Past hurts

When negative feelings arise because of past hurts, use your chosen technique to enter a meditative state (see Chapter 4) and imagine being in your peaceful place. When you feel sufficiently mellow, say or whisper the person's name and say, *I forgive you and release you to your highest good.* Another affirmation is: *I release all people, places, and things that must be released for my highest good.*

In case you need more releasing than can be provided by these affirmations, there is another releasing technique you can use, but it requires more time and effort. I call this the *letter to God.* (If you do not believe in God, consider it to be a letter to the earth.) Write a letter that nobody else will read, and irrevocably dispose of it while you are in a meditative or prayerful state. Using any writing medium and without mincing words, begin by telling the person(s) who hurt you anything you wish to say about your feelings and how his/her actions damaged you. If you believe in God or a higher power, express your frustration. Release the other person(s) to

God (or fate), with forgiveness of any apologies owed to you. Forgive yourself for carrying the hurt, and release it to divinity. State the resolution you want from the person who hurt you, including whatever apology and/or recompense you think is appropriate, and also state what the best possible resolution would be without such recompense. Affirm release of the obstacle and hurt regardless of the outcome, and ask for your *highest and best good*. Date it and sign it. (If you use a computer, print one copy and then delete the file from your computer.) Decide whether to burn it, shred it in a paper shredder, or tear it up into small pieces and dispose of it. Go into a light meditative state, pray if you wish, and say something such as: *I release these concerns to the Universe.* (You may release them to God, to Jesus, to any higher spiritual power, to your guardian angel or spiritual guide, or to the earth, to fate, etc.) Remember that forgiving does not mean condoning. Destroy the letter before you return to a beta state.

Intense past hurts *may require regression therapy* for full release. If you believe it would be appropriate for you, refer to the Q/A section in the Appendix for guidelines on how to choose a competent hypnotherapist. Also, ask any prospective hypnotherapist to explain his/her opinion regarding false memories. Anyone facilitating hypnotic regression MUST *be objective* and without any preconceived opinions. Otherwise he/she could taint the trance and leave you with false or distorted memories that could be mistaken for "repressed" memories. Be careful.

Some hurts that seem to be in the past might really have *current* unresolved issues that require resolution. If you require conscious resolution of a present conflict, refer to the exercises in the last chapter to keep your anxiety levels under control when you attempt resolution. Seek outside help if necessary. The need for such help is illustrated by a male client who once saw me in order to gain professional confidence. While practicing his releasing technique, he suddenly emerged from trance in tears. During his meditation he had attempted to relive several intense fights with his former wife. She was abusive to him as well as to their children; he was suing for custody. There are two lessons here: (1) just as a weightlifter starts working out with lighter weights before tackling heavy ones, we need to begin releasing smaller past pains before attempting larger ones; (2) some situations require professional help. I referred this man to traditional therapy.

Present hurts

If another person says or does something that causes us to indulge in negative thinking, we can apply the stress-coping technique (from Chapter 8). If we sink into negative thinking simply because of circumstances, or if we allow bad feelings to persist after using the stress-coping trigger, we need to do more releasing.

Since it is easier to talk about stopping negative thoughts than to do it, I include two mental exercises that may help release negative thoughts the moment they occur.

Remember the discussion about anchoring and triggers in Chapter 5? We can train the subconscious to respond to a signal that triggers our *freedom of thought!* Both of the following releasing techniques enable you to replace a negative thought with a positive one simply by giving yourself a signal. Let me emphasize that replacing is easier than erasing, especially when feelings dominate our minds.

The first technique involves use of the simple trigger established with the mental mini-vacation described in the last chapter. Whenever you feel negative thoughts taking root, it's time to activate your "inner peace" trigger and immediately fantasize your peaceful place. If necessary, practice the mini-vacation exercise several times to increase the power of your "inner peace" trigger. Also remember that the imagination is the rehearsal room of your mind. Fantasize the ability to go from a stressful situation immediately to your peaceful place, and to return to the present feeling calm.

The second technique expands on the first. Practice the stress-coping exercise along with your mental mini-vacation exercise. Then, either before or during your trance, recite the following two affirmations:

1. Whenever I use my peaceful-place trigger, I immediately imagine anything I choose.
2. My peaceful-place trigger instantly empowers me to use my best wisdom, knowledge, understanding, training, and experience to make wise decisions.

The peaceful-place trigger now serves two functions: (1) we can send a message of inner peace to the subconscious, providing at least some sense of calm; and (2) the trigger reminds us to make wise decisions! Perhaps we could fantasize the solution to the presenting problem. If that seems too difficult, then fantasize something totally different instead, and address the problem later.

Remember that any self-hypnosis empowerment *exercise* is the rehearsal before the performance. When negative thoughts try to invade the mind, it's *performance* time! Several rehearsals improve the performance. Once you have mastered the rehearsal, remember to use your peaceful-place trigger. If neither technique provides sufficient empowerment, you may also write the *letter to God* described above.

Additional Thoughts

If you succeed at releasing only a portion of the negative feelings, more work might be necessary. If past or present hurts squash your self-esteem, then seek counseling and/or hypnotherapy from someone competent to help you release the past and/or deal with present issues. While you may listen to the advice or opinions of friends or professionals, however, retain the power of choice for yourself. You must live with the benefits and consequences of your decisions, so do NOT *give away your power* (not even to a therapist). Any ethical therapist will help you gain more empowerment through problem resolution and healthy releasing.

The importance of releasing cannot be emphasized enough! Without release, the subconscious will stay trapped among the obstacles. I believe that's one reason why the world is filled with so much negativity and distrust.

We must stop energizing problems and instead start energizing solutions and their benefits. Instead of constantly looking back, we must frequently look ahead, planning our journey toward our goals. The following chapters that will help you do just that.

Chapter 10

Define and Celebrate Your Success

Are you ready to continue the journey? We must keep our eyes on the road ahead as we continue moving forward. How far do you think someone would get driving down a highway with his eyes glued to the rearview mirror 75% of the time? We easily accept the importance of looking at the road ahead and paying attention to road signs. Unfortunately, the journey toward our goals isn't mapped as clearly, nor do the directions make themselves obvious. When driving toward success, it's easy to get on a detour or to go off the road entirely, especially when definitions of success differ.

It is easier for the subconscious to follow our directions when we establish a course of action. Therefore each of us must determine his own definition of success. Whether you desire success in business or in other areas of life, you need to define what success means to you. Contrary to the opinions of those who put money ahead of happiness, success cannot be measured solely by the size of a bank account. Choose the right road for you!

What Is Your Definition of Success?

To many of us, success simply means doing what we enjoy and doing it well. To some, success describes an ongoing journey through life, filled with accomplishments. One can successfully reach academic goals, artistic goals, social goals, personal goals, social goals, religious goals, recreational goals, etc. There are many types of success.

Some measure success by the size of their bank accounts, but I have known wealthy people whose financial success resulted in sadness. Some self-centered achievers discover that their financial success is offset by total failure in love and happiness. Those who obtain success by sacrificing friends and family risk bankruptcy in the happiness department. Some roads to wealth glitter at first, but end in darkness. We can certainly welcome whatever financial successes we attain, but other goals can also be worth our efforts. Choose them wisely, because any success comes with a price and you must decide whether or not to pay it.

The first vital step in successfully reaching a goal is to become results-oriented. Choose the road you wish to travel, but first learn what waits for you at its end. Determine the goal's personal benefits. Imagine them often to help sell your subconscious on following your directions. (This approach is detailed in Chapter 13, along with an empowerment exercise.)

Next, determine the best method(s) of reaching your goal. (What kind of vehicle will you drive?) Whatever you have to do to realize your goal is its cost. Some people prefer to call the cost of success an *action plan*. Whatever the name, there will be tradeoffs. Very seldom will we find a goal simply handed to us without any effort on our part! Decide what you want and then go for it!

After you determine that a goal merits your time and energy, work toward bringing that goal to reality. As you progress toward the goal, realize that you deserve to enjoy your accomplishments, no matter how small they may seem. Look for them. Recognize them. Honor them.

Remember that, just as the driver will occasionally glance back in the rearview mirror, glancing back at our successes can be constructive. Allow me to explain.

Love Yourself: Celebrate Your Success!

Many clients from all walks of life have given me positive feedback about the benefits of the next self-hypnosis exercise. But before getting to it, let me provide some important preliminary information.

Just as we have the ability to replay tapes of past failures, we also have the ability to replay success tapes! Experience proves the value of remembering past accomplishments to reinforce both personal and professional confidence. Also, enjoying happy memories helps build self-esteem and self-love. Some people might ask: why should we learn to love ourselves?

If you genuinely like or love someone, you'll find yourself much more prone to do something good for him/her, even if it is *you*! How can we love others fully unless and until we love ourselves? Jesus instructed us to love our neighbor as we love ourselves. In our culture, however, it is a real challenge to find the proper balance in loving ourselves. Many people put so much energy into being good husbands/wives, parents, employees (or employers), citizens, Christians, "lightworkers," etc., that they get wrapped up in others and forget to love themselves! I call this the *forgotten half of the golden rule*.

If someone you love gets discouraged, would you criticize and make him/her feel worse, or would you try to say something *kind and encouraging* instead? The next time you feel discouraged, be kind to yourself by remembering your successes. It is important to take time simply to journey through these memories, reliving and celebrating them. Clients from all walks of life have enjoyed profound benefits from using the next empowerment exercise to make these journeys.

Empowerment for Peak Performance

I guide a client (or an audience) through an empowerment meditation process which I call "Celebrate Your Success!" or the *peak-performance meditation*. Clients enjoy this variation of a technique used and taught very effectively by Richard Zarro of Futureshaping Technologies (Woodstock, NY). The process involves establishing your own success trigger, or "power point," for success. To get the benefit from the exercise, carry it out *personally* rather than simply read about it; pay close attention to both the instructions and the script.

First, choose a gesture that will become your peak performance trigger. Some clients touch two fingers together, others squeeze a wrist. Touching my thumb to the palm of my other hand serves as my power trigger. A computer technician chose to pinch her earlobe. A professional singer decided to touch the backside of his tongue to the roof of his mouth, as he could activate this trigger without anyone noticing. Your peak-performance trigger should feel comfortable. (During the meditation you will make a decision the first time the script says "Activate your power point..." At this moment you may accept the trigger you consciously chose, or you may choose a different one.)

Next, choose an induction from Chapter 4. During trance, after counting down to your desired depth, imagine yourself in a safe place.

The script will guide you on a series of short journeys to various past successes: academic, artistic, athletic, professional, social, spiritual, etc. With each journey, use as many of your five senses as possible to replay the success in your imagination. Remember any and all of your *good emotional feelings*, and feel them again. Ignore any later criticism received from people trying to deflate the experience; think *only of the positive!*

Now, to anchor confidence and self-esteem into your peak performance trigger, activate your success trigger and imagine yourself in a special area for winners. It can be a "winner's circle" or anything you wish to fantasize, such as an Olympic podium, stage, or a temple. For example, a banker fantasized a temple with an angel awarding her a medal.. It's *your* mind; choose what you wish.

When the script projects you into a desired future success, activate your trigger again and imagine the same feeling along with the desired success. Remember that the imagination is the rehearsal room of your mind. Fantasize yourself at peak performance!

Notice that the empowerment exercise is in the *second person*. For best results, I recommend that you have someone read the script to you, or that you record it for your personal use only. (Comments in plain print are instructions and should not be read out loud.) If you wish to practice this exercise without hearing a recording, become familiar with the wording. Write down, on a 3x5 card or sheet of paper, a key word for each journey you wish to take.

Are you ready to begin? Choose your desired induction (from Chapter 4). Enjoy the trance state...

Now imagine yourself in your own safe place... You may come here in your mind whenever you wish to experience peace within...

Imagine beautiful sights, sounds, and feelings, which make you feel at one with nature. This is a journey of imagination. In the rehearsal room of your mind, you may rehearse or relive anything you choose. You may travel through time or space simply by imagining. In an instant you may imagine yourself in your favorite vacation spot... You may now return just as quickly to your own safe place... and as you imagine that inner peace, it becomes real...

In the storehouse of your mind is a record of everything you've ever experienced, including your successes and your triumphs... And as you allow my voice to be your guide, your inner creative mind will find that it is easy to re-create your accomplishments as you go deeper and deeper into the soothing state of hypnotic relaxation...

Now go back in time to an academic accomplishment and relive it in your imagination... Enjoy the accomplishment and appreciate the recognition... Activate your power point as you feel the feelings...

(Pause several seconds...)

Go to your winner's area...

(Brief pause during each visit to winner's area...)

Now come back to your place of peace, and take a deep breath, and go deeper... deeper and deeper. You are responding very well as you allow my voice to be your guide...

For your next journey you may choose a time when you enjoyed either an athletic or artistic accomplishment—a sports success or an artistic success... relive the experience with as many of your five senses as possible... Activate your power point as you feel the sensations of satisfaction and you create an attitude of gratitude...

(Pause several seconds...)

Go to your winner's area...

Now come back to your place of peace, and enjoy the increasing awareness that you may recall and relive your successes whenever you choose...

Now go back to a social success—a time when other people appreciated you... Activate your power point as you feel the appreciation... go deeper into the feelings of appreciation and into the awareness that it is good for you also to appreciate yourself...

(Pause several seconds...)

Go to your winner's area...

Now come back to your safe place once again, and take a deep breath and go deeper... deeper and deeper...

Now take a journey to a success involving job or career... Just BE THERE and relive the time of triumph... Activate your power point...

(Pause several seconds...)

Now go to your winner's area as you feel your increasing confidence...

(Pause several seconds...)

This VICTORY is ALSO a part of who you are, and you may remember your time of triumph whenever you choose...

(Brief pause...)

As you come back to your place of peace once again, you realize that we all appreciate a moment of special love or friendship from a friend or loved one. I want you now to go back to a totally pleasant experience when you appreciated an act of love... As you relive this experience, activate your power point and realize that you are worthy of love...

(Pause several seconds...)

We are asked to love our neighbor as we love ourselves, and that means it is good for us to love ourselves too... As you come back to your safe place of peace, go deeper into the realization that you deserve to love yourself... Feel the wonderful power of love transforming you into the best that you can be...

Now project yourself into whatever success you choose to imagine, and activate your power point... and imagine MAXIMUM SUCCESS!

(Pause several seconds...)

Feel the power of love, as you know that through the power of love you are free to celebrate your success! By loving yourself more, you love others more... and you find your life filled with greater love. By loving yourself more, you find yourself becoming more and more aware of your successes, both big ones and little ones... And all these suggestions are going into the storehouse of your mind, as you remember to remember your successes.

(Say the following with feeling and conviction...)

You have the freedom to enjoy even more successes. You have the freedom to love yourself enough to celebrate your successes... freedom to love yourself enough to be the person you choose to be.

(Pause briefly...)

The power of choice is yours, and like a muscle that's used becomes stronger with use, your power of choice becomes stronger with use... know it... feel it... OWN it! You love your power of choice, and this gives you greater confidence as you become more empowered to be the person you choose to be... free to be the best you can be... free to love yourself as you love others!

... And so it is.

Now, I am going to count from one up to five and then I am going to say "fully aware." At the count of five, let your eyelids open and you are calm, refreshed, relaxed, fully aware, and normal in every way.

One... Slowly, calmly, easily, and gently you are returning to your full awareness once again.

Two... Each muscle and nerve in your body is loose, limp, and relaxed, and you feel wonderfully good.

Three... From head to toe you are feeling perfect in every way... physically perfect, mentally alert, and emotionally serene... and when you get behind the wheel of your vehicle, you are totally alert in every way, responding appropriately to any and all traffic situations.

Number four... Your eyes begin to feel sparkling clear, just as though they were bathed in fresh spring water. On the next number now, let your eyelids open and you are then calm, rested, refreshed, fully aware, and feeling good in every way.

Number five... Eyelids open now. You are fully aware once again. Take a deep breath, fill up your lungs, and stretch.

[IMPORTANT NOTE: All the scripts in this book are copyrighted and intended only for the personal use of the purchaser of this book. If you wish to give or sell tapes to others, I have the peak-performance meditation on an audiotape with my award-winning voice. (Refer to the Appendix for details.) Any unauthorized distribution in any format without the written consent of the author will be considered an infringement of copyright. This script also appears on pages 216–219 of my book, *The Art of Hypnotherapy* (Kendall/Hunt Publishing) and appears here with the publisher's permission. One of *my* goals is to receive abundant compensation for my work, and including the above reminder about my peak-performance script will help insure that I achieve my goal as others benefit from this important empowerment exercise.]

Now, speaking of goals, let's talk about *your* goals...

Chapter 11

Choosing Goals

Would you consider not taking a map when you drive into an area where you have never traveled before? Would you drive from New York to Los Angeles without first choosing a route? Choosing goals compares to mapping your route through life's journey.

There are many books that emphasize the importance of setting, defining, and writing down goals. While goals provide an easy way of measuring success on life's journey, few people actually follow the experts' advice.

Some people simply believe that writing down their goals is a waste of time, but if you consider a goal worthy of your effort, doesn't it deserve the few minutes it takes to write it down? I recommend that you write down your personal and professional goals. A person once told me, *I don't need to write down my goals, because I already know what I want in life*. If we find reasons to avoid written goals, we may also find reasons to fail.

Let's return to the metaphoric automobile trip to Los Angeles. First you imagine being there, then you decide on a route. You may take the northern or the southern route, or you may take the shortest route. Once en route, there may be unexpected roadblocks and detours. You may encounter traffic delays, but you keep heading toward your destination. On the way you may take planned side trips to enjoy the scenery or to visit a special place.

Attainment of a goal may involve several methods to help you along the way—with one or more enjoyable (or not-so-enjoyable) activities, detours, or interim goals before arrival at the final destination.

The rest of this chapter presents simple guidelines to help you list goals according to types and categories, whether you define them as personal or business, and to help you arrange them in order of importance to your happiness.

Goal Types

There are four main types of goals: short-term, intermediate, long-term, and life.

Short-term goals are those that are realistically attainable within the near future, such as up to six months or a year from now. Examples of short-term goals might be to quit smoking, take off ten pounds, close an important business transaction, paint the kitchen, reach a monthly sales quota, or buy a new car.

Intermediate goals normally can be attained within one to five years. Examples of intermediate goals might include taking a trip to Europe, buying a new home, or changing careers. Some readers might already be in a position to take a trip to Europe on a moment's notice, so what might be an intermediate goal to one person could simply be routine to another. Buying a new car could be an intermediate goal to many people rather than a short-term goal. Opinions and personal preferences vary. It's your life, so you decide.

Long-term goals and life goals may be considered as major life-changing successes that normally take longer than five years to accomplish. Typical examples of long-term goals include: setting up retirement plans, putting the children through college, building a new home, and starting a new business. Many people wish to consider goals of two to five years as long-term, defining goals beyond five years as life goals. Again, you decide.

Goal Categories

Now that you have my definition of goal types, let's categorize them to help trigger your choices. My partial list of primary categories includes achievements, possessions, characteristics, projects, and changes. A goal could fall within more than one category.

Achievements are personal or business accomplishments you would like to enjoy. A personal achievement might be to put a child through college, to master an art or sport, or to sing solo for a church choir. A business achievement might be to reach a sales quota, to attain recognition for an accomplishment in your field, or to become a published author!

Possessions are things you wish to own, such as a new car. Owning your own business could be a short-term, intermediate, or long-term goal. Financial rewards could be the result of achievements, or they might be considered goals of and by themselves. You could put a financial goal in this category or in the first.

Characteristics are personality traits you wish to incorporate, or recognized professional titles. You might want to be more mellow, more confident, or more outgoing. You might want to have a position or a professional title. These, of course, could also be achievements, as most positions or titles (such as Ph.D.) have prerequisite achievements.

Projects could be something you wish to start or complete. Perhaps you started writing a book last year and wish to complete and edit your manuscript for publication. Perhaps you wish to assist with a church project, or get involved with the Chamber of Commerce. Maybe you would just like to remodel the basement to create a spare bedroom.

Changes normally involve habits, attitudes, or ways of thinking. Quitting smoking and/or losing weight require a change of habit. (Remember that once you learn something subconsciously you cannot simply erase it—but you can *replace* it.) Improving your golf game also involves changes of habit and attitude when you address the ball. If you imagine your ball going into the water hazard, guess where the ball will land! Instead, change the negative image to a positive one by imagining where you DO want the ball to go. Sports in particular often involve more mental imaging than most people realize. (Chapter 14 contains some exercises for sports enhancement.)

Some changes overlap characteristics. For example, learning to like yourself changes your attitude about yourself and others while giving you more positive personality characteristics.

Using the above guidelines to trigger ideas, list your goals on a sheet of paper. You may wish to use separate sheets for each goal type (short-term, intermediate, and long-term). Some people like to separate personal or family goals from career goals, but I prefer to mix them because anything important to my career is also important to me personally.

If your list has a total of fifteen or fewer goals, you may combine them in the exercise in the next chapter. If you have a substantial quantity, you may wish to do a separate exercise for each type.

Since most of this book addresses subconscious programming, some readers might ask why I devote this chapter to an exercise primarily completed by the conscious mind. Often we can best determine our top-priority goal by *accessing the subconscious* rather than by trying to decide through logic alone. Nonetheless, before using the subconscious to prioritize our goals, we must use the logic of the conscious intellect to create the list. If you haven't already done so, get your list of goals ready now.

After completing your list, you may wish to repeat a self-hypnosis exercise from Chapter 4. Simply go in and out of trance somewhat quickly. Then immediately after returning from the alpha state to full beta consciousness, look over your list and add anything new that comes to your mind. You might be surprised at what you add! Once you have established and defined your goals, you are ready for the exercise in the next chapter.

Chapter 12

How to Prioritize Goals

I designed this exercise to help you prioritize your goals by combining logic and feeling. Please read this chapter thoroughly before you begin the exercise, and make certain that you understand the instructions. Permission is granted to photocopy the chart on the next page for *your use only*, rather than to ask you to write in the book. (Any other copying and/or distribution will be considered copyright infringement.)

While these instructions may seem simple, many clients have failed to complete the chart correctly, so be sure to stay alert. You should be in a light alpha state (or just returned from one) while you are working on the chart, and you will have an easier time completing the exercise properly if you understand beforehand exactly what to do.

The concept is really quite simple: you will be comparing every goal you establish to every other goal, but *only once*. Ask yourself this question: *If I could achieve only one of these two goals, which one would I choose?* With each comparison you will make a choice, indicating that choice in the appropriate box on the form. The results determine which goals are most important to your happiness.

You will be able to follow the instructions in an alpha state only if you have already understood them while in a beta state, so be certain that you grasp the logic and purpose of this exercise before proceeding.

Now... are you ready?

Complete this exercise while in a relaxed state of mind. Individually compare goal #1 to every other goal. For each comparison [1 vs. 2; 1 vs. 3; etc.], indicate your preference by writing the number of the more important goal in the box where #1 horizontally intersects with the Goal x column. EXAMPLE: If goal #1 is more important than goal #9, write "1" in row 1 under column 9. If goal #9 has more importance to you than #1, write "9" instead. Note that many boxes are "X-ed" to prevent comparing the same goals twice.

SCORING: Count one point for each time you have written a preference for each goal. Note that I've simplified scoring by allowing numbers to appear ONLY in their respective horizontal or vertical rows (assuming you have completed the exercise properly). The goal with the highest score is your priority goal, and so on.

To assist you in understanding these instructions, the following pages contain a sample set of goals and a completed goal chart that you can use to follow the instructions.

Prioritizing Goals

Complete this exercise while in a *relaxed state of mind*.

Score	Goal	2	3	4	5	6	7	8	9	10	11	12	13
	1												
	2	x											
	3	x	x										
	4	x	x	x									
	5	x	x	x	x								
	6	x	x	x	x	x							
	7	x	x	x	x	x	x						
	8	x	x	x	x	x	x	x					
	9	x	x	x	x	x	x	x	x				
	10	x	x	x	x	x	x	x	x	x			
	11	x	x	x	x	x	x	x	x	x	x		
	12	x	x	x	x	x	x	x	x	x	x	x	
	13	x	x	x	x	x	x	x	x	x	x	x	x

Step 1: Numbering the Goals

List all of your goals. Number them in the order listed, without regard to type or category. If you have over thirteen goals, you may wish to segregate them by type (and renumber the segregated goals). If you still have over thirteen goals in a goal type, you may do one of two things: (1) extend the chart with additional numbers up to the total number of goals you wish to analyze, or (2) combine two similar goals. ("Trip to Greece" and "trip to Australia" could become "take a trip abroad.")

Step 2: Entering Self-hypnosis

Get comfortable and have the following items at hand: your list of goals, a copy of the chart, a pen or pencil. Enter self-hypnosis as you've previously practiced, but go only part way. When you feel relaxed, open your eyes and proceed with this exercise. You should be feeling somewhat mellow, even though consciously aware. If you go deep, bring yourself up to a lighter state. I actually recommend the latter if you feel stress for any reason. You might benefit from giving yourself a chance to unwind before beginning this exercise. Some people discover that simply listening to soft music helps them to feel mellow.

Step 3: Using the Chart

Place your numbered goals next to a photocopy of the blank chart. Notice the column of numbers going down the left side of the chart. In the left-hand vertical column #1 is your starting point. Read your own goal #1 and compare it with goal #2. Choose the more important of the two goals, and mark your choice by writing "1" or "2" in the box in the row to the right of #1 that is in the column below the #2 on the horizontal axis. (My sample chart indicates that goal #2 had more importance than goal #1.) Now compare goal #1 with goal #3 and mark your choice in the box below #3, etc. Compare your first goal with every other goal in this manner. After comparing goal #1 with each other goal, only the top line of the chart will be completed.

Now go on to goal #2. Compare it to every other goal, just as you have done for goal #1. Notice that you have one less box to fill in. Since #2 and #1 have already been compared, there's no need to have another box for comparing those goals again. (To make the chart easier to use, I placed an "X" on squares that will never be filled in.) Continue the comparisons until you have compared each goal to every other goal.

When you have completed this part of the exercise, each goal should have been compared *once* to every other goal you have listed (and your choice indicated in the appropriate box).

Sample Goal List

1. Buy new home
2. Revise book
3. Take trip to Greece
4. Enjoy abundant cash flow
5. Establish more branch offices
6. Establish average workweek under fifty hours
7. Pay off all debts
8. Take trip to Australia
9. Buy new computer system
10. Own a new car free and clear

Step 4: Making the Choice

There are two ways to choose between two goals, happiness and sequence.

The happiness method (previously mentioned) requires that you ask the question: "If I could achieve only one of these two goals, which one would I choose?" This approach gets into your gut feelings to help you determine the importance of your goals. I personally use and recommend this method most of the time.

The sequential method involves asking yourself, "Which of these two goals must come FIRST?" This more intellectual approach might be useful for deciding the chronological order in which you should work on goals, but does not lend itself to use with goals of mixed types—as short-term goals would normally come before intermediate ones, etc. There may be a time and a place for this method, so I include it.

Once you choose a decision method, be consistent throughout the entire exercise! The only exception comes when you find yourself totally undecided between two goals. Then you may break the tie by using the alternate method; remember to return to your original method for the next goal choice.

You may find it interesting to see how different the results can be from using each of the two methods.

Step 5: Scoring

Once you complete the chart, come back up to total conscious awareness by counting from one to five. Stand up and stretch to be sure you remain fully alert.

Now, count the number of times the number "1" appears in any box, and indicate the score in the column to the left of the chart. (Note my example on the next page. In my example, #1 appeared four times.) Now count all your #2's and do the same.

Continue until you've counted all the occurrences of each number. Remember to check every box. If you have completed the chart properly, each selected goal number should appear either in the column below its number, or in the row to the right of its number.

Step 6: Assigning Priorities

The most frequently chosen goal is your priority goal, and it should be listed as goal #1 on a new sheet of paper. Renumber and list the rest of your goals according to priority, with the highest score first, second-highest second, etc.

Break a two-way tie by reviewing the chart to see which of the two goals you chose when you compared them to each other during the exercise. For example, my goals #3 and #7 tied. Since I selected #7 when I compared #3 to #7, #7 is more important—even though they had a tie score of six. If you have a three-way tie, select either the most important or the least important of the three, then use the above tie-breaking method to determine the order of the other two.

Step 7: Evaluating the Results

Note my sample goal list in its new order of priority. Now legibly list your goals on a fresh sheet of paper so that your priorities will stand out clearly.

Review your prioritized list of goals. You may discover a surprise or two! Often a goal that you previously considered important comes out low on the list, and a seemingly unimportant one comes out high. Frequently, clients discover that a goal previously considered number one comes out below several others—and vice versa. Such surprises prove the validity of the exercise. I prioritize my goals in this manner several times each year, and am sometimes surprised at the results. Our goals change with time. You may find yourself updating old goals, adding new goals and, hopefully, deleting the ones that you have reached.

Prioritizing Goals

Complete this exercise while in a *relaxed state of mind*.

Score	Goal	2	3	4	5	6	7	8	9	10	11	12	13
4	1	2	3	4	1	1	7	1	9	1			
8	2	x	2	4	2	2	2	2	2	2			
6	3	x	x	4	3	3	7	3	3	3			
9	4	x	x	x	4	4	4	4	4	4			
0	5	x	x	x	x	6	7	8	9	10			
1	6	x	x	x	x	x	7	8	9	10			
6	7	x	x	x	x	x	x	7	9	7			
2	8	x	x	x	x	x	x	x	9	10			
5	9	x	x	x	x	x	x	x	x	10			
4	10	x	x	x	x	x	x	x	x	x			
	11	x	x	x	x	x	x	x	x	x	x		
	12	x	x	x	x	x	x	x	x	x	x	x	
	13	x	x	x	x	x	x	x	x	x	x	x	x

Sample Prioritized Goal List

1. Enjoy abundant cash flow
2. Revise book
3. Pay off all debts
4. Take trip to Greece
5. Buy new computer system
6. Buy new home
7. Own a new car free and clear
8. Take trip to Australia
9. Establish average workweek under 50 hours
10. Establish more branch offices

In Conclusion

Why should we invest time and energy in goals that do not contribute to our happiness and well-being?

I believe that the comparisons carry greater meaning when we involve our feelings as well as logic alone. Remember that the results are more likely to reflect your true desires if you use the happiness method. Entering an alpha state (or at least being mellow) will facilitate your ability to get in touch with your feelings. Knowing which goals provide the greatest happiness is almost as important as defining them in the first place.

If you are putting energy into a defined goal that has little importance to your own happiness—just because your conscious mind, your boss, or a loved one tells you which goal to work toward—then it is likely that you will encounter a certain amount of frustration. (Clients often buy into such goals because of the opinions of a family member, church, or an employer.) You can still choose to work toward that less important goal but, by putting equal or greater energy into your higher-priority goals, you can be happy as well as successful.

Accept your right to change your mind. Feelings can change with the circumstances. If, in six months, you repeat this session with the exact same goals, you may notice differences in their priority order. The new ranking may be the result of changes in factors in your life that influence your state of happiness.

Many people consider happiness to be a state of mind. One may attain intellectual, professional, and/or financial success while failing emotionally after fulfilling the wrong goals. In light of this, I highly recommend that you analyze both your intermediate and your long-term goals with the happiness method.

Also remember that success is doing what you enjoy doing, and doing it well. People who live in their own egos might try to judge your success only by financial results. Do you live to please them, or to discover your own full potential and happiness? A person earning an average income but totally enjoying life will attain far more success in the pursuit of happiness than a millionaire living in slavery to the demands and stresses of uncontrolled ego.

Know which goals are important for your happiness. Once you use this chapter to help you do that, plan your course and go for it!

P.S.: I accomplished most of the goals on my list. The ones not important for my happiness dropped off later goal lists.

Part Four

Creative Daydreaming

Chapter 13

Preparation

Once you identify your priority goal, it's time to prepare your subconscious to accept it and the method(s) you have chosen to achieve it. Simply knowing where you want to go won't get you there unless you take action. People often come to my office wanting a hypnotic magic wand to suddenly make them thirty pounds lighter. Hypnosis is not magic. A trance cannot replace a proven method to obtain results, but it can *motivate a willing mind to accept a proven action plan* by helping the subconscious to accept what the conscious mind has already decided to do. Without that acceptance, the inner mind may defeat us before we ever begin! Even when we have subconscious acceptance, we must still invest our time and energy—pay the price of success—because the universal law of *cause and effect* influences all of us.

Cause and Effect

Every action produces an effect; that is, the actions we take must be appropriate to the goal we want to achieve. The action plan, such as changing eating habits, causes the *effect*, or manifestation of the chosen goal. I refer to all necessary actions for goal achievement as the *price of success*. Although some readers might consider the word *price* negative, we regularly and willingly spend money for the goods and services we want. *Price* is negative only when it is too high.

Now let's explore further how the law of *cause and effect* applies to goal achievement.

Once we select a goal, we should use the logical left brain to determine what actions will cause our goal to become reality—to establish an *action plan*. If the price is too high (or the required action is too difficult), we might not wish to spend the necessary effort. You have the responsibility of determining the price and then deciding whether or not to pay it. Do you wish to motivate yourself to take the actions needed to reach the goal?

Many books describe ways of establishing an action plan to achieve various objectives: weight control, minimizing stress, sales techniques, study habits, body building, ways to hold a golf club, etc. Use any valid source to help you determine the course of action most likely to result in success.

If you wish to travel, you must know where you intend to go and how you intend to get there. If you were to set off on an automobile trip to Canada, would you just get in your car and head north? Unless you knew the roads, you would have to refer to a *road map* in order to plan the best route. Similarly, excellence in music comes neither by wishful thinking nor by self-hypnosis; it comes through paying the price of lots of practice! The same rule applies to any other art. Likewise, losing thirty pounds does not come from daily daydreaming in an alpha state. You must consciously program your subconscious to accept whatever eating and/or exercise habits you choose, and then execute the plan. The same holds true for any type of motivation or goal achievement. A salesperson cannot achieve a high sales quota simply by sitting in the office in an alpha state all day waiting for the telephone to ring; he/she must *do something*.

Since the action plan (or price of success) must be determined by your conscious mind, this book provides no specific advice regarding nutrition, salesmanship, tobacco withdrawal, etc. Instead, I teach people how to get the subconscious to buy into conscious decisions so that they can realize their goals.

Once you discover your best course of action and make the decision to follow it, you have your road map to success. Your next step is to convince your subconscious to accept it. Be prepared to *persuade* your subconscious to cooperate, lest you run into resistance. Get your imagination involved with the *benefits* of achievment by fantasizing them during self-hypnosis. I call this process "Selling Success to Your Subconscious."

Selling Success to Your Subconscious

We tend to resist a salesperson's efforts to force us into buying something. The same is true for selling motivation to the subconscious! Why do I call this process "selling"? Because we have all mentally tuned into station **WII-FM: What's In It For Me**? When you convince your inner mind of the answer, it will buy!

The subconscious tends to resist changing a habit simply because the conscious mind says so. Motivation is difficult at best until the subconscious bonds with the emotional desire to succeed. Our inner child might rebel against pressure, but it will respond to persuasion if the benefits are appealing. We might refuse to buy a fairly priced product when we are pressured to do so, yet how often have we paid more than we thought we should simply because we fell in *love with the product*?

The conscious mind must sell success to the subconscious by using the language of imagination. The subconscious resists giving up dessert, but will be comfortable (and happier) imagining the benefits of wearing clothes of an ideal size.

Once you have fallen in love with the benefits of your goal, greater motivation to implement the action plan follows; the key lies in persuading the subconscious to buy the *benefits* of change. Identification of the special benefits to you is, therefore, a precondition for successfully motivating the subconscious.

Before proceeding to the next chapter, list the benefits your priority goal will bring you. (Your subconscious responds better when you choose your own benefits rather than simply accepting someone else's benefits). Nonetheless, if your priority goal fits into one of the common exercises described in the next chapter, you may wish to select some additional benefits from some of those frequently chosen by my clients.

When you complete your list of benefits, you can marry two powerful methods of subconscious programming: *hypnosis* and *emotion*. Now you are ready to sell success to your subconscious; the next chapter will show you how!

Chapter 14

Creative Daydreaming Exercises

Now it's time to have fun.

Remember that alpha (hypnosis/self-hypnosis) opens a wide gateway to the subconscious, enhancing the imagination and creativity. Since imagination is the language of the subconscious, why not use the state of mind that increases our ability to daydream?

Emotion opens an even wider gateway to the subconscious. Remember that *emotion* is the *motivating power of the mind.* You become a servant to your uncontrolled emotions; controlled emotions become your servants. Emotional excitement about a goal motivates the subconscious and seems to add energy to get there faster, such as for an athlete trying to make an Olympic team. Accordingly, I've designed empowerment exercises to help increase your emotional desire to attain a priority goal.

I'm not talking about artificial emotional hype. Rather, we will use a process I call *creative daydreaming* to create positive, controlled emotion. It combines two powerful methods of subconscious programming to more than double their impact and far surpass the effectiveness of simply visualizing the goal. It's like putting high-energy fuel into your car and driving on a superhighway.

General Guidelines

This chapter serves as a reference and introduction to *creative daydreaming.* I encourage the reader to experiment with it at least once before leaving this book. You can add your key word and affirmations later—after you understand how to structure them properly.

Before you begin, choose one of the many common goals listed in this chapter, or another that you wish to work on, and list its benefits on a sheet of paper. (Refer to the last section of Chapter 13,: "Selling Success to Your Subconscious.") Amend your list whenever you wish. Sample benefits that clients frequently choose appear in the creative daydreaming exercises for popular goals below.

Remember that every invention and innovation originates in someone's imagination. When we enter the alpha state, we enhance our creative energies as well as our imagination. New ideas that originate in the subconscious and flow into the consciousness may contribute new methods of goal achievement that you had never thought of before, such as a way to simplify your action plan, thereby facilitating your ability to succeed. After emerging from trance, use logic to decide whether to use, modify, or discard any specific new idea.

If you are practicing creative daydreaming for the first time, proceed as explained in this paragraph and as described in the section related to your goal. For maximum benefit, please do not skip ahead. Review and refine your list of benefits. Memorize them, or at least become familiar with the main ones. Later chapters explain affirmations and key words, so don't worry about them the first time you practice creative daydreaming. Once you finish the book, refer to this chapter to help you practice; first take it one step at a time. You may ignore the next paragraph until after you understand *HypnoCise* (explained in the final chapter) and return to this chapter as a reference.

If you are using this chapter as a reference after completing the book, include your *properly constructed* personal affirmations in accordance with the instructions contained in the final chapter. Once you understand those instructions, read your affirmations out loud *before* practicing *HypnoCise*. Note that generic affirmations appear in the Appendix rather than in this chapter. From the list, select affirmations that are appropriate for you, or devise your own. Enjoy fantasizing your benefits, using creative daydreaming to make them personal. (Review the other guidelines in this section if necessary.) Incorporate your key word several times throughout your trance, especially when you feel good emotions. The energy of emotion helps to anchor your key word, thus adding strength when you use it as your empowerment trigger. During your creative daydreaming exercise, remember to fantasize successful use of your key word to maximize your benefits from *HypnoCise*; then use it in real life.

Now that you're ready, find a comfortable place and enter alpha as you have previously practiced. Once there, imagine that you have *already reached* your goal. Experience fulfillment of your goal. Imagine yourself seeing, hearing, and feeling the benefits you get from achieving your goal as *present reality*! Fantasize engaging in activities that become more enjoyable because of your benefits. If necessary, you may review your personal benefits, or have them memorized before entering the alpha state.

Get all five of your senses involved in what you imagine. Feel *emotional satisfaction* as you allow yourself to enjoy the fantasy! Imagine your appreciation of the benefits. As you fantasize your success in the rehearsal room of your imagination, fantasize your absolute ability to do what it takes to realize this goal! Imagine doing it successfully.

If you believe in a higher power, feel a sense of appreciation to God or to the Universe for making your goal possible. *Imagine an attitude of gratitude.* You are now building faith on a subconscious level, where faith gets results! As you begin to feel the positive emotions increase, imagine that the course of action you have planned becomes easy, and daydream doing whatever is necessary to realize the desired results!

Construct your meditation along guidelines similar to those described for one of the popular goals presented below. The benefits presented for each goal are those frequently identified by clients, and may help you refine your own list. Choose only those that *you* consider important, and include any others that you might enjoy.

While creative daydreaming enhances your subconscious desire to achieve a goal, some readers might encounter unexpected subconscious resistance caused by "old tapes." A competently trained hypnotherapist can help you discover the source of such resistance. (Refer to the Appendix for guidelines on how to choose a competent hypnotherapist.) This book is NOT intended as a substitute for hypnotherapy or other necessary professional help; rather, my goal is to give you a boost along your path to empowerment. If you are getting professional help, proper use of creative daydreaming may facilitate your ability to respond to it.

Now you can choose the exercise that best fits your priority goal. Enjoy it!

Smoking Cessation/Reduction

Common benefits for smokers wishing to quit or cut down are:

> *better health*
> *longer wind*
> *more energy*
> *more stamina*
> *more money*
> *greater social acceptance*
> *better self-image*
> *better professional image*
> *personal pride*
> *better complexion*
> *sense of accomplishment*
> *more freedom*
> *good parental example*
> *cleaner environment (car, home, clothes, etc.)*
> *whiter teeth*
> *clean breath*
> *better sense of taste and smell*

If you wish, add some or all of these benefits to your personal list. Once you are satisfied with your benefits, enter self-hypnosis using your chosen induction. Imagine yourself in better health. Your lungs reward you with more stamina and/or more energy as you imagine enjoying your favorite recreational activity. If you enjoy swimming, see the water. Hear the splashing and feel your body gliding smoothly as you swim. If you enjoy hiking, then see the surroundings. Hear the sounds of the great outdoors, and/or the sound of the laughter of your child or friend. Feel the warmth or coolness of the clean air. Imagine taking some of the money that formerly went up in smoke and spending it as *FUN money* because you deserve it! Imagine yourself in a social or professional situation. Imagine your other benefits with as many of your five senses as possible.

Choose rewards for your personal success, and imagine enjoying them. Take a deep breath and think the word *RELAX* (and/or another key word) for quitting or cutting down. Since replacing a habit is easier than erasing it, fantasize that *one deep breath* satisfies you more than an old light-up.

Imagine enjoying your new self-image as a nonsmoker (or occasional smoker). Fantasize your feeling of pride in or satisfaction with this personal success.

In real life, make a conscious effort to take one deep breath whenever any situation occurs that previously triggered an urge to light up. Be especially careful about the times when you might enter spontaneous trance, such as while watching television. The subconscious will have formed an emotional bond with the cigarette, so to break the old bond I believe strongly in the importance of bonding emotionally with your personal benefits. People who quit cold turkey (without totally selling the subconscious) could end up grieving for the loss of the "fair-weather friend" for months or years. You will make quitting (or cutting down) much less difficult by doing everything possible to make your decision enjoyable. Remember that quitting smoking is NOT an easy task for most people, even with hypnosis. You must make a total commitment to quit. Note the absence of affirmations in the Appendix; instead, I decided to include a full script for your use. If you have subconscious resistance, seek additional help.

Client Successes

Perhaps the most profound success I know of happened in the late 1980s in my college hypnotherapy class. I simply discussed the "Benefits Approach" (which I also call "Selling Success to the Subconscious"). One of my students then went home and listed his benefits. After using self-hypnosis several times to visualize them, incorporating the techniques presented in this book, he quit totally. He did NOT have this book to help him!

Another success that taught me something important occurred in 1986. A professional woman, who had initially indicated a desire to quit, continued seeing me because she wanted to smoke one cigarette after each meal. She then decided to stop seeing me, and waited almost a year before calling me again. When I received her phone call, she said, *I hope you don't think I'm a failure. When I first saw you, I had it in my head that either I had to not smoke at all, or be totally out of control. You taught me to take one deep breath instead of most of my smokes, but I enjoy having one cigarette for dessert after each meal. After ten months, I'm still at only four cigarettes daily ... one after each meal, and one before bed at night. Thank you for helping me control my habit.*

This businesswoman taught me how to facilitate *smoking reduction* programs for smokers who do not wish to quit. There is a smoking reduction script in the Appendix.

Weight Reduction

Common benefits for weight reduction are:

> *better health*
> *more energy*
> *more attractive*
> *greater freedom with clothes*
> *lighter on feet*
> *easier mobility (or freedom of movement)*
> *better self-image (social and/or professional)*
> *personal pride*
> *sense of accomplishment*

more sex appeal
more money

Note: People whose incomes depend on commissions and/or making a good impression often list more money as a benefit.

When you feel satisfied with your list of benefits, choose your induction (from Chapter 4) and enter self-hypnosis.

Imagine yourself standing in front of a mirror looking at a reflection of yourself at your desired weight. Imagine yourself enjoying your favorite activity while being at your ideal weight. Picture yourself wearing your desired sizes and styles of clothing and feel these clothes fitting comfortably on you! Imagine yourself enjoying the company of friends or loved ones while enjoying your ideal body. Feel a sense of satisfaction as you imagine doing things you enjoy. Imagine having more energy and being lighter on your feet. In your mind's eye, *be* on the dance floor or at the beach. Whisper your key word at appropriate times throughout your meditation.

Now imagine you have already been at your ideal weight for a *year*. Picture yourself buying that new outfit in your new size, and imagine it fitting comfortably! Continue this fantasy until you actually begin to feel excitement about the possibility of being there. Feel an improved sense of pride or satisfaction in your new image. Clients tell me that the reality surpasses the fantasy!

In real life, remember to *replace* snacks with a few sips of water. Trying to ignore snack urges could result in major backsliding! Additionally, take enough time to eat *slowly*, paying attention to each and every bite. Awareness of the taste of each bite of food will increase the emotional satisfaction you derive from what you eat, giving you more pleasure from fewer calories. Get in the habit of leaving food on your plate. (Would you rather have your food go to waste, or *waist?*) As with any goal, you must make a commitment to control your eating habits; remember that diets work on the body, but not on the mind.

Client Successes

Because she felt that a svelter image might improve her income, a professional consultant saw me for weight reduction. She was accustomed to leading rather than following, so I encountered considerable analytical resistance to trance. I saw her only three times, primarily emphasizing self-hypnosis techniques because of her apparent inability to get past a light state of trance. At the third session, I spent most of the time consulting with her on how to maximize her self-hypnosis; I gave her an hypnosis tape on empowerment for weight management. One year later, an attractive and slender woman approached me in a restaurant. At first I failed to recognize her, but she took my hand and introduced me to her husband. He said, "So this is the man you take to bed every night!" After my face turned several shades of red, the three of us laughed loudly. Since I can't help all the people all the time, I must admit that her profound success surprised and pleased me. She later saw me for help with another goal.

A devout Christian decided to try hypnosis as a last resort. Unfortunately, she consumed over a quarter pound of chocolate candy nightly! She taught me that it's not *what* we eat; rather, it's *how much* and *how often*. This client needed to take off about thirty pounds, but she refused to give up her chocolate. She cut down to only two pieces of candy nightly, and made minor modifications in her other eating habits. Although she spent seven months reducing, she minimized subconscious resistance by avoiding diets; she simply changed her eating habits. As far as I know, her success is permanent.

Sales/Business Motivation

Identifying business benefits can sometimes be a two-step process. The first step is to identify your direct benefits. My professional clients often identify many of these direct benefits:

> *more money (higher income, etc.)*
> *security*
> *promotion*
> *recognition*
> *performance award(s)*
> *greater prestige*
> *pride of success*

The second step involves identifying those benefits related to financial success. Most people in business are strongly motivated to earn greater income and need to list the benefits from it. Complete the second step by identifying what money can do to improve your life. Clients most frequently choose the following:

> *new home*
> *new car*
> *new furniture*
> *new boat*
> *put child through college*
> *get advanced degree*
> *freedom to travel more*
> *vacation to (destination)*
> *be debt-free*
> *more free time*
> *new (whatever)*

First, after entering self-hypnosis, imagine your direct benefits. Fantasize receiving a promotion and/or a professional award. Imagine a feeling of security in ways that you consider important. Since money itself is a direct benefit, imagine holding a large check in your hands, payable to *you*! Imagine depositing this money into your account. Fantasize the deposit slip and/or the bank balance. Whisper your key word.

Next, imagine your related benefits of a greater income in vivid detail! Be personal, using as many of your five senses as possible. For example, don't just think of a new car as two words. Instead, imagine yourself in the driver's seat. *See* the interior and exterior. *Hear* the purr of the engine or sound of the stereo. *Feel* the wheel and the comfort of the seat. *Smell* the new upholstery. Imagine yourself putting the pink slip in a safe place, indicating to your subconscious that *you own* the car. (One of my clients simply imagined driving a new car; he rented a new vehicle while his car visited the repair shop!)

If you desire a new home, see it inside and outside in your mind's eye. See the living room. Feel the carpet. Imagine hearing the voices of loved ones inside this house. Imagine eating and relaxing here, etc.

Does a luxury cruise appeal to you? Imagine yourself sipping champagne or tropical juice on the deck of a ship while you smell the salty sea air. See the sea and hear the sounds. See, hear, and feel anything pleasant that you anticipate with this experience.

If you strongly desire more money, imagine yourself holding a wad of crisp, new $100 bills. What would you do? What would you buy? How would you feel? Let your imagination run free. (One of my clients got a wad of one-dollar bills and put a $100 bill on top and bottom. He felt the money while doing his self-hypnosis, imagining all as $100 bills. This fantasy helped renew his motivation for sales.)

Finally, fantasize your feeling of dignity gained as a result of your success!

Client Successes

The most surprising success in this department occurred when a successful salesman saw me when he was already earning a six-digit income. (I did not reveal to him that I envied his income!) Naturally, I taught him the techniques presented in this book. One year later he informed me that he had almost doubled his income utilizing my techniques.

My most encouraging business success brought tears of joy to my eyes. A physician referred to me for stress management a patient who worked for a company that took unfair advantage of its sales force. (Having gone through a similar experience, I had great empathy for him.) After having him use *creative daydreaming* to envision his benefits, he realized that he needed to change employers. Although I explained that he might benefit from talking with a vocational counselor, he chose to work on confidence and self-esteem first. He also mastered the stress-coping technique presented earlier in this book. Two months later he accepted a position with another company at a base salary *twice* his previous income *plus* commission!

Job Performance

Self-hypnosis to improve your job performance is similar to the exercise described above for business motivation. Identify your direct benefits (similar to business motivation benefits) as well as the related benefits if your income will improve as a result of better job performance. Enter trance, using your chosen induction. Fantasize your personal benefits with as many of your five senses as possible. Include your related benefits. If you simply wish to feel good about your current job, consider all the things your paycheck allows you to buy, and identify the benefits of receiving regular paychecks. During trance, fantasize those benefits even if you already experience them. With either situation, fantasize yourself performing well on your job. Rehearse it in your mind, with as much detail as possible. Remember to use your key word.

Those who wish to change careers may need more help than this book can provide. Seek appropriate professional help if necessary.

Client Successes

After selling her old business, a self-employed woman moved across the country to the Pacific Northwest. Even after consulting with a vocational counselor, she could not decide whether to start a new business or seek employment. She listed a dozen prospective new careers as goals and used the goal-prioritizing exercise detailed in Chapter 12. Her "priority goal" became her career choice; she became successful and happy.

Memory and Study Habits

If improving study habits involves motivation to complete your assignments, identify and list your own specific benefits for keeping pace with your academic goals and objectives. Common benefits are:

> *better grades*
> *graduation*
> *promotion*
> *better job*
> *degree*

Fantasize those benefits during the trance state. Imagine holding a good report card in your hand. Visualize receiving your award, certificate, or diploma. Feel the handshake. Hear any associated sounds, such as "Pomp and Circumstance." Imagine any opportunities for career advancement made possible by your accomplishment. Make the benefits *real* in your imagination! Selling your inner mind on the *benefits of successful studies* will increase the motivation needed to do your homework. Remember to use your key word.

For *test anxiety*, master the mental mini-vacation exercise described in Chapter 8. Your peaceful place trigger will help calm pretest anxiety. During your creative daydreaming, imagine *successfully* using that trigger just before an exam, and imagine a high score! Next time you find yourself taking a test, remember to use your peaceful-place trigger.

If your concern involves the ability to concentrate during your scheduled study time, you might need to seek help beyond this book.

Client Successes

My most profound success resulted from a simple hypnosis demonstration at a high-school psychology class. The teacher asked me to demonstrate hypnosis in the classroom; after she produced signed parental consent slips, I agreed. During the demonstration, I gave affirmations for memory and study habits. One year later the same teacher invited me back, and told me a success story. Apparently one of my earlier volunteers had been a D student. The next semester the former D student got a 4.0 GPA and obtained the highest scores of any student in the psychology classes taught by this teacher. Faith at a subconscious level gets results.

Miscellaneous Habits

To overcome undesired habits, identify and list your own personal benefits as previously instructed. Enter trance, using your chosen induction. As in the above examples, vividly fantasize your benefits, using as many of your five senses as possible. Create scenarios in which you enjoy your benefits. Whisper your key word at appropriate times.

IMPORTANT: If you have a difficult habit to break, seek professional help. Even with traditional therapy, however, you might find creative daydreaming helpful in maintaining the motivation to put into practice any advice given by the therapist. If in doubt, show him/her this book, so that any of its self-hypnosis exercises can be individualized to your specific needs.

Client Successes

In 1990 an attorney entered my office and said, "I want you to help me overcome my Coke habit." As I started to refer him to a substance-abuse counselor, he interrupted me rather quickly. He apologized and explained that he meant Coca-Cola! Simple use of the benefits approach helped him sell success to the subconscious. He substituted water part of the time, and decafe coffee part of the time.

Over the years, clients have asked me to help them cut down on drinking cola or other soft drinks. Crystal-Light in moderation may be an acceptable substitute.

Motivational Goals

Motivational goals can fall into any of the goal categories mentioned in Chapter 11: achievements, possessions, characteristics, projects, or changes. If your priority goal requires motivation and does not appear elsewhere in this chapter, then identify and list your personal benefits, whether your goal is to achieve political office, remodel the kitchen, write a book, participate in a church project, or go into business for yourself. Ask yourself a question: *What do I get from this goal?* (Remember WII-FM from Chapter 13.)

Client Successes

A career woman asked me to help her increase her motivation to keep her house clean, as she wished to set a good example for her children. Although I asked her to list her personal benefits, the subconscious can often become quite creative! Her new way of solving her concern surprised both of us. She decided to hire a housekeeper to do the major portion of the housework, paying for it by working overtime. She decided that having the work done was far more important than trying to do it herself! Although she could have reached this decision consciously without ever seeing me, the idea came instantly during trance. Sometimes the obvious comes much more readily from the subconscious than from the conscious mind.

Confidence/Self-esteem

My experience with clients leads me to believe you will find the *peak performance* meditation to be the best starting point for building confidence or self-esteem (see "Celebrate Your Success," Chapter 10). You may also incorporate affirmations for confidence and fantasize *being the person you choose to be*! Depending on your needs, outside help for confidence and/or self-esteem may be necessary. Note: if you have not yet finished this book, choose a motivational goal for your first creative daydreaming exercise.

Client Successes

A professional speaker whom I respect greatly emerged from trance giving me a strong emotional appeal. I had facilitated an earlier version of the peak-performance meditation for her. She looked at me as though she could see right into my soul and said, *This is too good to keep hidden in this office. You must get this out into the business world!* While I respect her confidentiality, I'm grateful for her encouragement. She told me that numerous successful people need more confidence and self-esteem.

Sports Enhancement

Unlike habits and professional goals, sports enhancement frequently does not involve motivation. Usually we simply wish to *improve* our skills and/or our consistency. Where improvement requires increased motivation to practice, creative daydreaming helps regardless of the nature of the sport.

Sports such as running and swimming primarily involve physical fitness and endurance. The athlete wins primarily through endurance, fitness, and strength rather than mental skill, and the mind must focus on victory. Other activities, such as golf, are far less physical, but all sports involve the mind far more than many athletes realize! Even basketball, which requires great physical stamina, could be classified as a mental sport as well as a physical one. Baseball players most certainly recognize the importance of keeping their eye on the ball! Just ask a pitcher whether or not confidence and concentration can influence pitching skills. Football players, who must become very fit physically, quickly discover how attitude can influence a game.

General Guidelines

Motivation frequently becomes necessary only for the person who finds it difficult to practice often enough to attain his/her athletic goals, regardless of whether the sport is primarily physical or mental. If you fit this category, then list the benefits of staying motivated. Do this in a manner similar to the previous exercises in this chapter, selling your subconscious on the benefits of staying motivated. Schedule a regular practice time and stick to it! During your creative daydreaming exercise, fantasize the benefits of mastering the sport, as well as the pride of accomplishment. If your goal involves becoming (or remaining) professional, imagine the desired championship and/or the benefits of compensation. You may also imagine successful participation in the activity itself. Blend in your key word as appropriate; say it to yourself at the times you set aside to practice your athletic activity. Your word to trigger motivation will be different from the performance trigger used to enhance skills and actual performance.

Enhancing sports skills can be accomplished best through understanding and using triggers for peak performance. (Refer to Chapter 5 to review the section on *anchoring* and *triggers* if necessary.) Practice again the exercise for peak performance described in Chapter 10, exclusively remembering several past successes involving sports. *One deep breath* accompanied by thinking the word *focus* will generally be your best trigger for enhancing peak performance in sports; you may also add your other peak-performance trigger (power point) for extra empowerment if you wish, making it an alternate *sports trigger*. Anchor your past athletic successes into your sports trigger. During your activity, you may use the word *focus or* your power point (or both) as a trigger for peak sports performance.

For more specific guidelines in some common sports, refer to the appropriate subsection below. If you already participate in professional sports, you may find it worthwhile to invest in a few private sessions with a competent hypnotherapist for sports enhancement. A properly trained hypnotherapist can help you work through any specific weak areas that might be influenced by your subconscious. (When choosing a hypnotherapist, remember that, unless you also have psychological problems to resolve, experience in the use of hypnosis is more important for sports enhancement than a background in psychology.)

For each of the following exercises it is important to determine those specific areas in which you desire improvement in skills and confidence. Upon entering trance, take a deep breath, imagine yourself in the specific situation you want to improve, think the word focus and/or activate your power point, and then fantasize successful application of the desired skill.

Archery/darts

Feel yourself holding the bow and arrow (or dart). See the target. Imagine hitting the bull's-eye! Next time you engage in this activity, use your key word (or sports trigger) at each turn just before launching the arrow or dart.

Baseball

Determine those specific areas (batting, fielding, pitching, or catching) where you desire improvement in skills and confidence.

Batting: Fantasize *several* times at bat. Imagine hitting the ball squarely for a single, or for a double down the line (or in the gap). See the pitcher. Feel the bat in your hands. Hear the sound of bat meeting ball as you swing it. If you need to improve your bunting skills, do so in your mind's eye. Make it vivid! Now imagine hitting a home run. Remember to use your trigger before each exercise in your mind. In the real game, use your sports trigger when you step up to the plate.

Fielding: Regardless of the position you play, fantasize yourself fielding the ball to the best of your ability. Remember to use your sports trigger as you practice creative daydreaming. In real life, use your trigger as each new batter steps up to home plate.

Pitching/Catching: Just before each pitch, fantasize exactly where you wish the pitch to go. If catching, practice moving the mitt as needed to catch each pitch. In your mind, practice throwing out a runner trying to steal second base. If pitching, think the word *focus* and fantasize all the right motions. See the ball going precisely where you wish.

Basketball

Determine those specific areas (free throws, lay-ups, jump shots, three-pointers) where you desire improvement in skills and confidence. Imagine the sounds of the crowd and/or the ball bouncing on the court. In the actual game, you will be able to use your key word before making free throws, but you might be too busy running up and down the court at other times to think of it. Use your sports trigger with each time out, before each jump ball, and before each free throw (regardless of who makes the shot). Should you feel yourself losing concentration at any time during the game, use your sports trigger during a momentary pause.

Bowling

Determine those specific areas (first ball, single-pin leaves, 7-10 splits, etc.) where you desire improvement in skills and confidence. Fantasize rolling the ball appropriately. Feel the follow-through. Hear the ball land. See it hit the pin(s). Next time you bowl, remember to use your sports trigger just before each frame and/or second ball.

Football

Determine those specific areas (offense, defense, special teams, passing, receiving, etc.) where you desire improvement in skills and confidence. Imagine yourself catching the pass, making a touchdown, breaking a tackle, making the tackle, etc. Fantasize all the sounds and feelings as well as what you can see in your mind's eye. During the game, use your sports trigger just before lining up prior to each play. If you need help in specific areas for confidence or attitude, invest in private sessions.

Golf

Prior to entering trance, identify the specific skills you wish to improve. During your creative daydreaming exercise, fantasize successful application of these skills. Just before each imagined application, activate your sports trigger; then fantasize success. See the examples below.

Tee: Do you wish more distance off the tee, more accuracy, or both? In your imagination, BE at the fourth hole (or seventh hole) of your favorite golf course. Fantasize placing your tee into the ground. Pick up your golf ball. Feel it in your hand as you place it on the tee. Reach for your driver or desired iron. Imagine *details*! Now use your sports trigger, and then imagine properly addressing the ball. In your mind, swing the club! See and hear the club connect with the ball. Feel the follow-through. Imagine the ball flying perfectly through the air, touching the fairway, rolling and landing exactly where desired.

Fairway: Do you wish to use a driver and/or iron accurately on the fairway? In your imagination, BE on the fairway. See the lie of your ball. Look at the green in the distance. Reach for your club and use your sports trigger for peak performance (as above). Imagine the ball landing exactly where desired.

Chipping: Imagine yourself chipping onto the green in the same manner as the above examples. Use your sports trigger and imagine the ball landing exactly where desired.

Putting: Reach for your putter in your mind's eye. Use your sports trigger. Imagine the ball rolling perfectly and dropping into the cup. See and hear the ball drop. Do this exercise several times with the ball at various distances from the cup.

Difficult holes: You may fantasize getting par or a birdie at a difficult hole simply by going through each stroke as in the above examples. Remember to fantasize using your sports trigger for peak performance just before each stroke. Once you actually get to the golf course, *use* your trigger as practiced in your mind!

Gymnastics

Determine those specific areas (parallel bars, rings, etc.) where you desire improvement in skills and confidence. Go through the entire routine in your mind, from start to finish. During actual practice or performance, whisper or think the word *focus* just before beginning your routine and/or activating your power point.

Physical sports (swimming, track, etc.)

Determine those specific areas where you desire improvement in skills and confidence. If you need more motivation to practice, list your benefits as described previously. Fantasize victory. During the actual competition, use your sports trigger while approaching the starting line.

Skiing

Fantasize yourself getting ready to go down the slope. Fantasize beginning your downhill run. If you know the particular slope you wish to master, go through it from start to finish in your mind. See the snow in front of you. Feel yourself making the appropriate movements as you glide downhill. Hear the sounds in your mind's ear. Make it real! If you wish to prepare for a competition, use creative daydreaming at least once nightly (or daily) for at least one entire month before the competition. During the actual competition, take one deep breath and think the word *focus* (and/or activate your power point) just before beginning your run.

Soccer/hockey

Determine those specific areas (defense, offense, goal tending, etc.) where you desire improvement in skills and confidence. Imagine making a goal. If you tend the goal, fantasize various blocks.

Other sports

Determine those specific areas where you desire improvement in skills and confidence. For example, if you engage in competitive diving, fantasize the entire dive from start to finish. See it in your mind. Feel your body making the desired moves. Hear the sounds as you hit the water. During the actual dive, take one deep breath and whisper or think the word *focus* (and/or activate your power point) just before diving. For skating, fantasize your entire routine in your mind, from start to finish. Use these same guidelines for other competitive sports.

Client Successes

A golf semiprofessional invested in four sessions before a golf tournament. In the first two sessions, I used the techniques presented in this book. During the third and fourth sessions, I mentally took him over the entire golf course, having him rehearse every stroke. He placed among the top five in the tournament.

A swimmer wanted to place in the top ten and saw me primarily for motivation to maintain his practice schedule. I also taught him to use the peak-performance trigger as his sports trigger; he won the bronze in an international competition.

If Your Goal Isn't Included Above...

Read the rest of this book and apply whatever you consider useful. Practice self-hypnosis, incorporating creative daydreaming along with your affirmations and key word. Fantasize total achievement of your desires. Seek professional help if needed.

If your top-priority goal does not fit in any of the basic ones above, to help you appreciate the value of this self-help book you may wish to practice creative daydreaming about a lesser goal that is included in this chapter. Remember to add your affirmations and your key word.

When Might Hypnotherapy Be Needed?

This book has several recommendations to seek outside help when necessary, yet some readers might wonder how they would know *when* to seek hypnotherapy. Using self-hypnosis is like using mental muscles. Some changes require only easy "lifting" that you can make without any help. Other changes require removing a mental block (subconscious resistance to change) that can be more easily achieved when someone else guides or helps you. If I move a chair by myself, it's easy, but if the couch needs to be moved, it's much easier to move it with someone else's help.

Self-hypnosis can empower you, to varying degrees, primarily in the common goals presented in this chapter. Even if you consult a professional, you may derive enough benefit from the empowerment exercises alone to help you go the full distance. When motivation is the primary need, this book will pay for itself many times over provided you practice self-hypnosis for empowerment.

Give yourself several weeks to work on a specific habit or motivational goal, utilizing all the relevant exercises explained in this book. Within a month it should become quite clear whether the subconscious wishes to cooperate or resist. If the subconscious indicates only minor resistance to change, you should be rewarded for your patience. If the resistance persists, the need for outside help should become obvious.

While you are probably the best judge of knowing whether you need a hypnotherapist, the following paragraphs present some indicators that might signal the need for outside help. (If in doubt, you may wish to refer to Chapters 5 and 6 to estimate how many subconscious motivators oppose your goal.)

Smoking cessation/reduction: Within two or three weeks of quitting, you should notice at least a 50% reduction of both the frequency and severity of urges.

Half of the smokers contemplating quitting might need more help than this book provides. Remember that the subconscious accepts a new response to an old trigger much more readily than any efforts to erase the trigger. One deep breath has no calories and no side effects. Additionally, you may wish to do some of your own research into other related aspects, such as physical withdrawal from nicotine. Seeking hypnotherapy might make your struggle easier; the choice is yours. Even with outside help, the empowerment exercises in this book should provide valuable assistance.

Weight management: Your attitude toward food should change within a few days, although your body might wait longer to reflect the changes in your weight and figure. You should feel more motivated to reduce. Strong inner conflicts indicate a probable need for outside help. Lack of satisfying progress would be another clue that you need additional help. Whether or not you seek outside help, I strongly urge *you* to accept responsibility for doing your own research into proper nutrition. No hypnotherapist (or counselor) should consult with you on nutrition unless he/she can prove having received specialized training in nutrition. With questions or concerns regarding nutrition and/or physical exercises that might be appropriate for you, consider the wisdom of consulting a licensed health care professional trained to help you in those specific areas. Some physical exercises may be good for some people and dangerous for others. (One of my clients saw me for weight management because her personal physician recommended hypnosis to help her become motivated to follow appropriate medical advice. Her physician also recommended *against* all exercises except walking because of her heart condition.) Use wisdom when you plan your course of action. If you have any concerns about nutrition or exercise, please consult with the appropriate licensed health care professional first; use self-hypnosis and/or hypnotherapy as an *adjunct* to your weight-reduction program.

Business motivation/job performance: Your attitude should improve within days after practicing the creative daydreaming exercises, especially when you enjoy your work. If your job fails to provide satisfaction, consider talking with a vocational counselor. Hypnosis will not make you like a job that you hate; it will help you become more willing to do the unpleasant tasks that help provide benefits that you deem important (such as a weekly paycheck). If you truly hate your job, then seek vocational counseling rather than hypnotherapy.

Memory and study habits: Some of my clients have enjoyed profound improvement simply by using *HypnoCise*. Depending on the cause, self-hypnosis may provide help ranging from almost total success to no noticeable improvement. If the memory problems are related to physical health or serious emotional problems, even hypnotherapy may not be sufficient. Other professional help from either a mental health professional or licensed physician will be needed, depending on the cause of the memory problems. If you feel that there is any possibility of a physiological cause, consult with your physician. If you have major unresolved stress (family, marital, etc.), your memory problems might be a symptom of those unresolved issues. You may need to consult with a professional for assistance. If memory problems are primarily related to a lack of motivation and/or to test anxiety, hypnotherapy may be the best answer.

Sports Enhancement: Self-hypnosis really shines here! Unless an athlete suffers a serious confidence problem, mental imagery can help greatly to improve existing abilities, especially when combined with the sports trigger. You would most likely require hypnotherapy only if you desire more intensive help, or if the subconscious wants to hang on to stubborn resistance.

Self-hypnosis can also help in varying degrees with the other goals mentioned in this chapter. I recommend that you remain aware of your progress in order to determine whether or not you need extra help. The primary question to ask yourself with any goal is: *Am I making progress, or does my subconscious block most of my efforts?* If you believe the latter to be true, seek outside help.

While you might still derive benefit from some of the empowerment exercises in this book (such as the ones for reducing stress), releasing heavy subconscious resistance normally requires assistance from someone competently trained. I believe in both self-hypnosis and hypnotherapy, but an ethical hypnotherapist also knows when to refer a client to another professional.

Certain problems usually require outside assistance from a hypnotherapist and/or from another professional. Among these are: phobias, unresolved grief, serious self-esteem issues, posttrauma stress, health problems (illness or injury), alcoholism or substance abuse, obsessive eating disorders, obesity, chain smoking, depression and other serious mental, family, or relationship and vocational problems.

Normally, an ethical hypnotherapist will help you with pain management only after medical referral. Some of the other issues mentioned in the above paragraph may also require help beyond the scope of hypnotherapy. When the problem has possible physical causes, seek a licensed health care professional. When serious emotional trauma and/or ongoing abuse contribute to your problem, seek traditional mental health care (or traditional therapy). When the problem can be resolved with simple subconscious programming, you may choose either self-hypnosis or hypnotherapy (or both). You can look in the Appendix to find guidelines for choosing a competent hypnotherapist.

Are you ready for Part Five now?

Part Five

Adding Words of Power

Chapter 15

How Words Impact the Mind

Effective self-hypnosis requires a basic understanding of how words impact the mind, especially when one or more of the subconscious gateways may be open. Additionally, good affirmations (positive statements of belief) can enhance a trance, adding more power to your experience.

Do you remember Emile Coue from the history chapter? He taught *autosuggestion* to all who would listen. Just as hypnotherapists refer to Mesmer as the father of hypnosis (a title shared by two others as well), we can consider Emile Coue the grandfather of self-hypnosis. While most practitioners of hypnosis took the role of *hypnotist* who tried to put subjects "under their power," Coue—a man before his time—sought to help people become *self-empowered through autosuggestion!* Autosuggestion then gave rise to affirmations, but they remained in the embryonic stage for decades. Though they are similar forms of suggestion, autosuggestion is usually used only during a trance state, whereas affirmations may be used at any time, and whether or not the user believes in the benefits of trance. This chapter revolves around a very important similarity between affirmations and hypnotic suggestions: *both enter the subconscious!*

During the '60s, I saw very little material recommending the use of affirmations. My friends and work associates all shunned autosuggestion in any form. Now there are many religious books that recommend the use of affirmations; just check the bookstore in any Unity Church or Church of Religious Science. Nevertheless, some churches consider affirmations to be "bootstrap" methods (try to pick yourself up by pulling on your own bootstraps). The church I formerly attended frequently used this metaphor to discourage the use of affirmations and autosuggestions.

Affirmations finally became more popular in the '70s and '80s, but all too few practitioners seem to know how to properly structure and use them. Used wisely, words become powerful tools to help us create motivation and success attitudes in the subconscious. If misconstructed or misused, however, autosuggestions and affirmations can actually move our goals farther from reach. We must be cautious when using affirmations.

Sticks and Stones

Remember the old saying, "Sticks and stones may break my bones, but words will never hurt me"? It is my professional opinion that *inappropriate words can and do hurt us* when a subconscious gateway is open. Allow me to illustrate from my personal experience.

When my first marriage broke up, my sales hit rock bottom even though I had previously enjoyed success. An insurance executive told me: *Nobody does well in sales for two years after a divorce!* This negative idea entered my mind like a powerful hypnotic suggestion. I was still taking the same actions as in prior years, but without results. My financial strength vanished quickly enough to send me into a near panic. My income dropped to a small fraction of its previous level, leading me into overwhelming debts. Self-help books no longer helped, and I kept wondering why. Today I know what happened. During the crisis of divorce, my subconscious believed what the insurance executive had told me—and that belief remained in my subconscious. My mind replayed that executive's statement like a broken record, and it became a negative affirmation. I received a double whammy, because this statement originated from a professional authority figure and entered my subconscious through the gateway of authority as well as the gateway of emotion.

Here are some other examples that resonate with many people.

A mother exclaims loudly to her child, *Don't spill the milk!* The glass often gets tipped over within seconds because the child's mind immediately creates an image of spilling the milk.

Parents often tell their children, *Don't forget your coat!* Need I explain what happens? Next time, simply tell your child: *Remember your coat.*

A golfer says, *I'm not going into the water,* and where does the ball land? This same concept applies to other sports as well. For example, during an important at-bat in a baseball game, a teammate says, *Don't strike out!* How often does the feared strikeout arise?

A dieter says to a friend (or self), *I'm not eating any dessert at this party!* yet later reports *either* eating dessert at the party *or* eating dessert at home after the party. Someone I know attempted to control her eating habits with affirmations such as *I don't like sweets any more.* Does that statement make you imagine something sweet? Her subconscious responded by increasing her consumption of chocolate.

A well-known corporation encouraged salespeople to tape a 3x5 card to the dash of their car with the following statement: *I don't quit until it hurts!* Upper management expected that affirmation to remind each representative to make just one last call at the end of each day. In reality, however, that statement gives the subconscious two very negative messages: (1) prospecting hurts; and (2) when it does, you can quit! Indeed, one of my clients quit a good sales position because of the damage done by this affirmation. By the time he saw me, he was earning a lower income in a less desirable company.

During my successful years in the insurance industry, management told me: *Everyone has call reluctance; it comes with the territory.* Even now, many salespeople accept this as their reality! Sales management school taught me that nobody likes to make prospecting calls, but prospecting is the *cause producing the effect* of secured appointments.

Many firms create a "success formula" that can also serve as an affirmation. Here's the one that I taught my agents: *Thirty calls daily equals ten interviews weekly equals three sales per week.* I personally used this prospecting formula (and its affirmation) to generate a good income for almost a decade. Reflecting on my sales career, however, one constant jumps out at me: Whenever I expected a sale, I usually got it; if I expected to lose the sale, the result met my expectation.

The Law of Expectancy

This subheading could just as easily be called: *The Principle of the Self-Fulfilling Prophecy.* This basic natural law means that we tend to get whatever we believe or expect at a subconscious level. My late mentor, Charles Tebbetts, taught that we can help empower our clients by helping them change what the subconscious expects; the results of fifteen years of private practice validate this opinion.

Affirmations, hypnotic suggestions, and/or autosuggestions should be constructed to convince the subconscious mind of the possibility of what the conscious mind already accepts. I recommend that we choose affirmations that take advantage of the law of expectancy, and avoid making statements to ourselves that create a negative expectancy that actually becomes counterproductive. Choose your words wisely.

While I'm not a family counselor, I would recommend that even parents heed this advice when giving parental commands to their children. We frequently tend to emphasize *unacceptable* behavior, as in *Don't talk back to me!* rather than the *desired* result. What usually happens?

The consequences of this kind of statement lead me to another important law of the mind.

The Law of Reversed Effect

For some strange reason, the subconscious tends to ignore negative statements, causing the imagination to focus on the reverse. In my profession we call this the *law of reversed effect.* To illustrate it, have a friend read the next paragraph to you:

Take a deep breath. Close your eyes and relax. Now, you MUST NOT think of a dog!

How did you respond? In your imagination, did you *see, hear,* or *pet* a dog? Most people almost immediately imagine one. When you tell the mind NOT to do something, it creates the fantasy of what is to be avoided. I'll explain further.

A smoker wishing to quit usually thinks *I can't have a cigarette; I don't want one anymore.* This self-talk usually results in a nagging desire to imagine how good one would taste or smell, and the craving increases until he/she replaces the fantasy of a cigarette with a totally different fantasy. Untrained hypnotists often tell people, *You don't like chocolate now. Sweets and junk food simply don't appeal to you anymore.* Does this make you imagine chocolate or some other junk food? You must replace the undesired image with a different one.

A client who went through one of those quick-fix stop-smoking programs listened to the audiotape she purchased, and then wondered why she gained forty pounds in nine months. At her request, I listened to the hypnosis tape. One of the hypnotic affirmations was: *You do not need food as a substitute for smoking.* You guessed it! She wanted hypnosis to stop her from substituting snacks for cigarettes!

The Law of Awareness

Another law of the mind is called the *law of awareness*. In simple terms, this law means that you tend to attract whatever dominates your mind. As you put mental energy into the problem, you tend to magnify its effect at a subconscious level, attracting circumstances that could intensify the very problem you wish to overcome! Consequently, it is imperative to use affirmations that *focus the subconscious on the desired results* rather than on avoiding the problems. This law goes hand in hand with the law of reversed effect.

Many of our state governments promote the statement: *Don't drink and drive.* Have you wondered why so many drivers ignore that statement? The subconscious hears (or reads) those words without the negative. Furthermore, this authoritative statement puts one's awareness on the problem rather than the solution, thus creating the image of drinking and driving. The effect is more severe when television opens the alpha gateway to the subconscious. A better message would be: *Drive sober.* The best ad that I ever saw regarding alcohol and drinking focused on the solution. The narrator said, *The man in this car is too drunk to drive...* The scene showed headlights on a foggy night, with the car parking and depositing a passenger. The next statement was: *That's why he took a cab home.*

Remember that any statement designed to enter one of the subconscious gateways serves like an affirmation—whether spoken by you about yourself, or spoken by somebody else when your subconscious is receptive. As I said before, choose your words wisely.

Be Careful What You Say

During my time of trial, I read a self-help book that gave numerous examples of affirmations about avoiding fear and eliminating poverty. The basic concepts and ideas seemed logical to my conscious mind, but negative results cropped up like weeds in a field! The author of that old self-help book used incorrect wording; the more I used the affirmations, the more they hurt me. At the time, I did not know why. In the same way many of my clients have learned the hard way to avoid common negative statements. Wise King Solomon said that there is life and death in the power of the tongue, so we must choose our words wisely. Careless use of negative statements just might cause them to enter one of the subconscious gateways with adverse results. Consider the risks of statements such as:

> *That makes me sick.*
> *That gives me a pain in my —.*
> *That job was a major headache.*
> *I'm going to finish this if it kills me.*
> *That almost gave me a heart attack.*
> *That will be the death of me.*
> *No pain, no gain.*
> *Fear is a mind killer.*
> *That was a back-breaking job.*
> *That tears me up inside.*

That burns me up (or makes my blood boil).
He (she) is driving me crazy.
How can I be so stupid (dumb, ignorant, etc.)?

Have you found yourself using any of these negative statements frequently? Only time will tell whether or not these (or similar) statements can influence the subconscious to cause negative things to happen to us.

As a hypnotherapist, I now understand the importance of semantics when dealing with the subconscious. Affirmations are like hypnotic suggestions (because they enter the subconscious) and must be constructed similarly, but stated in the first-person format. Remember this fact as you read the next chapter.

Chapter 16

Choosing Your Affirmations

Using the guidelines presented in this chapter, choose several affirmations that support your number one priority goal. Some people prefer to write their own affirmations; others would rather find some that already exist. Either is acceptable as long as each statement contributes to the desired results.

Affirm the Desired Result

Remember the law of reversed effect? Positive statements motivate the subconscious much more effectively than negative ones. For example, if you say *I am not afraid to speak in public*, your subconscious mind ignores the "not"—and you still claim the fear. A better way of stating this proposition is: *I am a confident public speaker*.

Amazingly, many professionals inside and outside the hypnotherapy profession focus on the problem to be avoided rather than on the solution. Some hypnosis scripts available for sale contain many negative suggestions that often reinforce the problem.

Examine the statement: *I am in control of my temper*. This simple sentence sounds harmless enough, but what awareness does it create? Does it remind you of a time when you got angry? Rather than claiming ownership of a temper, why not claim a calm disposition instead? A better way of stating the proposition would be: *I am a calm person*.

On the rare occasion that it becomes necessary to state a problem in order to affirm the solution in the same statement, state the problem in the past tense and put the solution in the present tense. Remember to put your awareness into solutions as well, as in the following example: *Whenever something occurs that used to push stress buttons, I take one deep breath and remain calm—totally in control of my feelings.*

You can affirm your desired results in three areas: *journey, destination, and attitudes.*

> **Journey:** *I am a person who exercises daily.*
> **Destination:** *Exercise keeps me energetic and physically fit.*
> **Attitude:** *I enjoy exercise and appreciate its benefits.*

The journey serves as a symbol of your course or action plan. The destination is your goal fulfillment, including the benefits. You may also affirm positive attitudes about both the benefits and the price of success—such as an attitude of gratitude.

Now let's discuss some other important guidelines for choosing (or writing) your affirmations.

Present Tense versus Future Tense

If you give your subconscious an escape hatch, it usually takes advantage of the opportunity. Examine the following statement: *I will control my eating habits*. This statement contains no trigger to activate the action; it is open-ended. We all know that tomorrow never comes. The subconscious, however, might get worried and say, *Eat, drink, and be merry, for tomorrow we diet!* The affirmation could be rephrased as: *I make wise choices about my eating habits*.

Sometimes doubts prevent a present-tense statement from obtaining subconscious belief. For example, an obese client might not comfortably say: *I am slender and attractive*, because the subconscious knows otherwise. We can effectively bypass this problem by making a slight modification: *Each day I am becoming slimmer and more attractive*.

Even though the conscious recognizes this proposition as only a future possibility, present improvement is implied; the statement rests comfortably in the subconscious.

For many years I avoided all other uses of the future tense, until I learned about some research done by Arthur Winkler, Ph.D., who has hypnotized more than 34,000 people. He used the future tense in many hypnotic suggestions—without subconscious resistance. His linking of the suggestions to a specific time or event as the trigger for the action apparently makes a difference to the subconscious.

Use Active Words

I can sing. Does that statement tell you that I actually do sing? I can also cook—when I get around to it. (God bless microwaves!) *Can* is a passive word. If you want to affirm ability, then you may use *can* in your affirmation; however, *active* statements carry more power than passive ones. For example: *I CAN improve my memory* does not carry as much strength as: *I AM improving my memory each time I use it*.

Many hypnotherapists (including me) use more permissive suggestions with *can* simply because the subconscious will more readily accept an indirect suggestion from an external source than it will a direct one. However, when we state our own affirmations, the direct approach normally works best. Rather than trying to be fancy, just be direct and specific.

Be Specific

The subconscious knows no jokes, so we should leave no room for error. We must state our desires with simple, clear, and specific words. For example, examine the next statement: *I am losing my excess weight*.

Can you find the subconscious escape hatch here? During childhood, others programmed us to *find* what we had lost! How many people keep losing weight, only to find it again? One client told me that he had "lost and found" over one thousand pounds during a ten-year period! We can reduce, take off, release, discard, get rid of, give away, throw away, eliminate, or donate excess pounds, but using the word *lost* sends a message to the subconscious to try to find it again! Say: *I am reducing regularly, until I reach my ideal weight.*

My mentor encouraged his students to keep the language simple enough for a child to understand. Since the subconscious responds much better to simple language, I agree totally. Some people seem to thrive on long, ambiguous affirmations with big words; if the conscious mind has difficulty understanding the statement, it's a sure bet that the subconscious will also be confused.

Now let's examine two powerful words: *I am.*

These two words contribute toward self-empowerment; use them often in a positive way! Affirm how you think, act, and feel about the reality of your goal as well as your method(s) of attainment, and affirm your benefits as well. For example:

I am a nonsmoker now.
I am enjoying the right amounts of the right foods.
I am more energetic at my ideal weight.
I am self-motivated.
I am thankful for my increasing success.
I am more confident with each passing day.

Bear in mind that goals *must be believable to the subconscious* in order for "I am" statements to be effective. If you don't believe in your ability to reach your goal, then choose some affirmations that will contribute toward that belief.

If you wish to write your own affirmations, remember to be specific, keeping all your statements in the present tense unless linked to a specific trigger of a time or event. (*I am becoming more confident every day* rather than *I will be confident.*)

Remember the laws of the mind discussed in Chapter 15 as well as the guidelines presented above. Review them as often as necessary. Please understand the importance of this advice before attempting the final empowerment exercise, as reaching your goal may depend upon it!

If you prefer, you may import affirmations written by others. For your convenience, the Appendix contains affirmations for various goals. Please feel free to use whichever ones you wish, making whatever changes you want. Also, feel free to reproduce the affirmations for *your personal use only.*

Why Use Affirmations?

Good affirmations help convince your subconscious of your ability to reach your goals and to pay the price of success. Simply using creative daydreaming about your benefits would be like finding that car you wish to buy, only to discover that nobody is willing to tell you how to buy it!

Frequent positive statements can also help you become self-motivated, since motivation and subconscious beliefs frequently become intertwined. Your affirmations are the posthypnotic autosuggestions that you will be programming into your subconscious; that's why I place so much importance on their structure. Remember that you may affirm your benefits, your journey (or action plan), and your attitudes about your goal.

Are you ready to move on now? If so, you may choose from existing affirmations or write your own, following the guidelines above. In either case, pay close attention to the rest of this chapter.

Edit Your Affirmations

Once you feel satisfied with the affirmations you have written and/or chosen, I recommend that you edit them before you use them. Given below are some examples of improperly written affirmations, all of which other professionals have recommended in speeches or in writing! Note how and why I edit them. At the end of each paragraph, I give the better way of making the statement:

#1: By avoiding sweets and junk food, I am losing weight.
Try not to think of a dog … and what happens? This affirmation violates the law of reversed effect. Furthermore, it put awareness into sweets and junk food. Personally, it makes me imagine potato chips. You might think of pizza, pie, or candy. Next, this statement reminds me of the old saying, "Finders keepers, losers weepers!" That sends a message to the subconscious to go looking for what was lost. Let's simply say: *My good eating habits help me attain and maintain my ideal weight.*

#2: I hate smoking because it harms my health.
This statement affirms the problem rather than the solution. Worse yet, it also affirms health problems! I can't help but wonder how many people may actually develop health problems because of the excessive attention given to the hazards of smoking. Even those who manage to quit might easily find themselves feeling very uncomfortable in the presence of people who still smoke. Let's state the desired solution: *My lungs reward me for the fresh air I give them. I am a tolerant nonsmoker.*

#3: I easily forgive people who hurt me, understanding their weakness.
Over the years I've used this poor example of an affirmation many times because it contains hidden negative messages. If you decided to use it, you would affirm that other people hurt you, but that's okay, because other people are weak and don't measure up to your standards. This statement could easily become a path to self-righteousness. A much more positive statement is: *I am a forgiving and understanding person. I am tolerant of other people's opinions.*

#4: I love objections, and each NO gets me closer to the next sale.
Are you a professional salesperson? If so, avoid this statement like the plague. The problem is simple: if you love objections, you will most certainly get them! Furthermore, you'll think of them as objections to buying rather than concerns of ownership. Many sales organizations, including the one that formerly employed me, teach their sales force to use this statement. The logic is to help salespeople put a value on each interview, since no salesperson bats a thousand. But the subconscious receives negative messages. If you use this statement as an affirmation, your subconscious might alter your presentation to attract objections! I've advised many salespeople to rephrase the statement as follows: *I give wise responses to customer (or client) concerns because they move us closer to the best decision. I accept that each interview has value regardless of the final decision.*

#5: I will be out of debt by xx/xx (month and year).

This statement is personal, because I discovered its flaws the hard way. First, unexpected setbacks (such as car repairs, illness, etc.) may delay the target date. Second, if the target date approaches without the goal coming into sight, it becomes more difficult to believe, resulting in increasing stress. Worse yet, this statement leaves the method of debt clearing totally open. In my case, I made the mistake of using this affirmation verbatim (lifted from a self-help book) and specified January 1984 as the time for being out of debt. Bankruptcy was NOT what I had in mind! I learned the hard way to use the following statement instead: *My increasing money supply replaces past debts. I am grateful to God for my increasing abundance, and I am becoming more confident with each passing day.*

I'll share another mistake from my past...

#6: I always have enough money to pay my bills.

Where's the extra money left over to pay *yourself?* Some of you probably play "credit card bingo" by transferring balances from one credit card to another. I know what it's like to borrow from VISA to pay MasterCard; the results can be very costly and depressing. This statement is better: *My income continues to surpass my expenses.*

Financial concerns plague many millions of people worldwide, so I'll include one more example of a dangerous affirmation regarding money.

#7: I see myself depositing $XX,000 into my account.

One of my clients followed the advice of a seminar leader who recommended making out a deposit slip for $10,000. The facilitator instructed him to visualize making that deposit and to repeat the above statement every day for thirty days. Within one month after following that advice, a lawsuit settlement required him to liquidate some real estate in a forced sale, netting just over a third of the actual equity. You guessed it—he got just over ten thousand dollars, when he should have netted almost $30,000! It's better to affirm something like: *I have $XX,000 in divine ways that are good for all concerned.*

#8: I am not afraid of speaking in public.

Before reading further, try your hand at rewriting this affirmation:

_____

_____

_____

_____

Which two laws of the mind did the above statement violate? How close did you come to my revision? *I am becoming a more confident public speaker every time I speak in public.*

If you are still unclear, then I suggest you reread both Chapter 15 and this chapter. Now let's take a look at one of the most ambiguous affirmations that I've ever seen recommended publicly. . .

#9: I realize that we are NOT our body, actions, or awareness and that blame and guilt are NEVER valid because any fault in what we do lies NOT in us but in our faulty awareness.

Can you believe that I lifted the above statement verbatim? Use your new skills to decide what to change:

_____

_____

_____

_____

These few examples represent only a very small sample of poorly written affirmations recommended by "experts." We must remember that whenever a subconscious gateway opens, the subconscious accepts statements literally. Subtle wording, often overlooked by the conscious mind, can alter or reverse the meaning of an affirmation. Choose your affirmations carefully, whether you import them or write them. Then, before using them, edit them carefully. Once you believe that your affirmations are ready, I recommend two more important steps:

1. While feeling mellow or while in a somewhat relaxed state of mind, review your affirmations slowly and carefully. Add any new ones that occur to you. Delete or change any existing ones that do not feel comfortable to you.
2. Add your key word as described in the next chapter.

Chapter 17

Adding a Key Word

To benefit from repetition, many professionals recommend reading or saying your affirmations many times each day. I prefer using a subconscious trigger. Rather than repeating one or two affirmations a hundred times daily (as one self-help book advocated), you can simply choose one word or phrase that, to your subconscious, represents an entire group of affirmations. You will, therefore, only have to spend time with your affirmations when you do your self-hypnosis. You can use your trigger the rest of the time.

I call this trigger a *key word* because it acts like a key to the subconscious. I recommend that you give your priority goal a key word and add it to your list of affirmations:

My key word is _____. Whenever I say, see, think, or hear the

word _____, it automatically reinforces all of these affirmations.

Let's explore some reasons for this recommendation.

Many people involved in network marketing practice what is commonly called treasure mapping for success. The treasure mapper places a picture symbolizing the goal in a handy place (e.g., the refrigerator door). The symbol could be a picture of oneself at an ideal weight, a tropical beach, a new car, etc. The picture becomes an automatic, subconscious trigger (see Chapter 5) to follow the action plan for goal achievement. Key words work much the same way—and better with people who do not visualize well. Furthermore, you can have several key words, with each word representing a different goal.

We all carry a set of keys to unlock doors. I have a set of key words that unlock certain doors of my subconscious mind. For example, the word *relax* means that I am calm, confident, and in control of my feelings. The word *money* reminds me that money is a tool empowering me to express greater love and enjoy greater freedom. The word *love* serves as a master key, linking all of my business, personal, and spiritual affairs to the win/win attitude.

Start by selecting a key word for your priority goal.

Choosing the Best Word

Your key word should feel good emotionally as well as make sense intellectually. Smokers wishing to quit or reduce smoking normally choose the word *relax* as their key word. One deep breath usually accompanies the key word as a way of replacing an undesired habit with a new one. If you prefer, you may use the word *free* or *occasional* if you choose to smoke occasionally.

Many clients have chosen one of these key words for weight management:

slender
slim
attractive
satisfy
shape
sexy
healthy

One man tried *self-discipline* for his key word, but his subconscious rejected it. The child inside the subconscious does not like discipline, and my client had to choose a new word. Another client chose *get buffed* and found his subconscious quickly rejecting it because the phrase brought back painful memories. Make certain your key word *feels* good!

For sports enhancement, I normally recommend the word *focus* as the best key word.

Clients typically choose key words like these for confidence, success, or sales motivation:

confidence
success
client
money
abundance

Clients wishing to improve memory and/or study habits frequently choose:

remember
memory
grades
mind

These samples should help you choose a key word that suits you, even if neither your goal nor a good key word appears here. Select a positive word related to your goal. Then sit back, relax, and take a deep breath. Close your eyes and ask yourself: *Do I like this word as my key word?* You should have a feeling of either *yes* or *no*. Once you feel satisfied with your word, write it down.

How to Use Your Key Word

Although your last affirmation should define your key word, you may find it helpful to include it with several other affirmations. For example, if you choose *satisfy* as a key for weight reduction, you might say: *Nutritious foods satisfy me physically, mentally, and emotionally.*

The final empowerment exercise shows you how to incorporate your key word into your subconscious to enjoy its maximum benefit. You must then accept responsibility for using it frequently. The benefit to using a common word is that you will find yourself using and hearing it many times a day; each time it will act like a trigger at your subconscious level.

You might consider putting the affirmation containing your key word on a card that you keep on your refrigerator, vanity mirror, desk, or car dash—anywhere you will see it frequently. You can also make a point of saying or thinking your word often, until you're well on the road to reaching your goal.

Now that you have your list of benefits together with your affirmations and key word, are you ready to attain your ideal self-empowerment? Go to the chapter on *HypnoCise*; use it in your life.

Chapter 18

HypnoCise

Are you ready to magnify the effectiveness of your empowerment exercises? Let's blend self-hypnosis with key words, affirmations, creative daydreaming, and positive emotion. I call this technique *HypnoCise*. To the best of my knowledge and experience, this is the most powerful and creative self-hypnosis motivation technique available. Get ready to use your completed list of affirmations and personal benefits.

Review

In **Part One** we explored the purpose of this book, the various states of the mind, what happens when we enter the alpha state, and how to prepare for altered states. We dug a little into the history of hypnosis. By practicing the simple relaxation techniques described in Chapter 4, you got some exposure to self-induced hypnosis, even if you attained only a light state. By becoming familiar with the feeling, you increased your awareness of other trances you encounter during the day—such as staring out the window and daydreaming!

Part Two discussed why and how we need to program the subconscious. To understand how the subconscious is influenced and to avoid possible traps, we traveled through the five subconscious gateways. Because emotion is the motivating power of the mind, we practiced *important* stress-reduction exercises that help us control emotion. The mental mini-vacation meditation provides an inner peace trigger, and the technique for falling asleep has been a godsend to some of my clients. We discovered how you can at least choose your response to stressful circumstances. We demonstrated how practicing stress management exercises can benefit you in both your business and personal life.

Part Three presented help for clearing obstacles from the road to our goals. We showed how releasing negative attitudes and becoming aware of past successes can empower us to work more easily toward a goal. Because of the power of imagination, we demonstrated how to learn from past mistakes without dwelling on them. You also learned how (and why) to list your goals, and discovered a way to prioritize them using a combination of logic and feeling. We showed how important prioritizing is to choosing the right roads to success and happiness.

Part Four discussed the law of cause and effect and why it is important to identify and list the benefits we anticipate from achieving our priority goal. We showed why you must evaluate the price of success and decide upon a course of action. We investigated ways to greatly increase subconscious acceptance of the goal and its price by first getting our emotions involved with the benefits. We demonstrated the need to fantasize, through creative daydreaming, your sense of emotional satisfaction at achieving your goal. Chapter 14, which you can use as a reference source, introduced empowerment exercises for reaching various common goals.

So far in **Part Five,** we have discussed the power of words and why we must structure affirmations properly. Self-hypnosis works as quickly and easily as you can daydream, especially when combined with positive emotion. Together, imagination and emotion make a good marriage. We have showed how combining these two methods of programming with your affirmations makes your affirmations work much faster. Unless you have not yet done any of the empowerment exercises, you should already have a key word chosen for your priority goal. If not, then go back and review the chapter on key words and make a temporary selection before proceeding.

Now let's put everything together and master *HypnoCise!*

Doing It!

As with every empowerment exercise, you should read the instructions through more than once—often enough to become familiar with what to do when you put the book down. Follow the steps outlined below:

1. As in previous exercises, get comfortable. Have your affirmations and list of benefits in hand. If the exercises described in Chapter 14 covered your priority goal, you may expand upon those instructions by including all the steps described in this chapter. At your option, you may use mellow background music, but avoid music with distracting lyrics.

2. Review and memorize your benefits. Although you may open your eyes to refer to your benefits, using the conscious during trance may bring you partially up out of alpha. I also recommend memorizing your benefits so that they become a *part of you.*

3. Read your affirmations slowly. Linked to your key word, your affirmations become autosuggestions. Even if your mind tends to wander, you should keep reading them one word at a time. Reading out loud helps slow you down because you have to read each word. You may also wish to fantasize each affirmation as you read it, provided only good feelings emerge. If any subconscious resistance surfaces as you read, practice the creative daydreaming exercise several times *without* reading your affirmations. Selling success to your subconscious will later cause it to become more receptive to your affirmations.

Should you choose to use one of the scripts provided in the Appendix, include your affirmations at the appropriate places in the script.

4. Repeat three times a reading of the affirmation designating your key word. This exercise will help anchor your key word and affirmations together into your mind so that your key word becomes a trigger for your goal.

5. Remove glasses, contacts, etc., and enter alpha using one of the inductions previously learned. Takes steps to minimize any probable distractions, such as from a dog, cat, ringing phone, etc. Ask your family members to avoid disturbing you. When you feel mellow and easily able to fantasize, continue to the next step.

6. Daydream your benefits using as many of the five senses as possible (as in the creative daydreaming exercise). Make your daydream *vivid*.

7. Once you feel yourself becoming emotionally involved in your benefits, think of your key word. You may say it several times in your mind, or even say it aloud. You do not need to open your eyes to review your affirmations, because, at a subconscious level, your key word now represents all your affirmations, transforming them into autosuggestions. This process is second only to hearing someone else give you the affirmations as hypnotic suggestions. (If you wish, you may play your pre-recorded, *second-person* affirmations at this time. See "Tips for Success" below.)

8. Imagine that you have already achieved your goal! Review your benefits again. Imagine doing enjoyable things when the goal is realized. *Be there* in your imagination! Fantasize your appreciation of realizing your goal, and allow yourself to be open to any new, potentially helpful ideas that flow into your conscious awareness from the creative part of your mind. Remember that the alpha state helps you become more creative as well as imaginative—but keep it positive. Keep a notepad handy to record your new ideas. If any negative thoughts creep in, replace them. Remember that you cannot delete negativity simply by *trying not to think of it*. The subconscious prefers to replace a negative thought rather than to erase it, so replace the problem with the solution.

9. Establish a method of waking up. You may lose track of time. The alpha state is so pleasant that time can easily expand or contract depending on your perception and thoughts. Losing track of time is what professionals call *time distortion;* it happens, for example, when we get engrossed in a movie. Your mind can also wander, causing your perception of time to change. As with each empowerment exercise, you might wish to set an alarm. Some clients also tend to drift into the theta state while doing their self-hypnosis exercises. If you feel yourself drifting close to sleep, you might actually wish to open your eyes to read your affirmations a second time. Then close them and daydream your goal as explained above.

10. Bring yourself back to full conscious awareness. When ready, *slowly* count from one to five and open your eyes. If you use a music tape as background, you may wish to give yourself the autosuggestion of awakening when the tape ends.

NOTE: If you attempt to awaken yourself too quickly, you could find yourself feeling the same way you would feel if suddenly awakened from a nap.

11. Now that you have a key word, use it! Put a 3x5 card with your key word on it in a location where you will see it several times daily. Find other ways to see, hear, or say your key word frequently.

After understanding the above instructions, you may refer to Chapter 14. Its empowerment exercises will take on new meaning. Remember that *HypnoCise* includes (but is not limited to) creative daydreaming.

Tips for Success

Practice *HypnoCise* regularly until you find yourself automatically motivated to reach your priority goal, then use the same tools to help yourself reach other important goals. You will find that your ability improves with practice, just as your muscles strengthen with physical exercise. Nonetheless, just as a couch moves more easily with someone on the other end helping you lift, you might reach some goals faster with the help of a hypnotherapist.

You may wish to record your affirmations in your own voice to play back during your *HypnoCise* sessions. If so, you should record them clearly and slowly using the second person so that your subconscious hears them as though you were hearing hypnotic suggestions. For example, *I am* statements become *you are* statements. You may wish to state your benefits into the recorder (example: imagine having *more energy* while you enjoy your favorite activity, etc.). You can even include your induction and wake-up instructions as long as you record them in the second person. (Note that the scripts provided in the Appendix are already in the second person.)

Remember the five subconscious gateways. It is easier to avoid motivation pitfalls than to get out of the pit afterward. We can also look for possible ways to incorporate all five subconscious motivators into additional motivation tools (refer to Chapter 7).

While using any subconscious-programming tool, make certain you monitor what enters your mind. You must guard your thoughts when the subconscious gateways are open, and especially guard your imagination! If you do not filter out the garbage, you may still find yourself manipulated by others. By being aware of the times your subconscious is open and vulnerable, you encounter many more opportunities to take real control of your life.

Remember: *Imagination is the language of the subconscious* and *emotion is the motivating power of the mind*. Keep your focus on the desired results, and imagine the emotions you will enjoy upon attaining your goal. Rather than worrying about the price of change, fall in love with the *benefits* of success! Then frequently use your key word as a subconscious trigger for success. If you follow this advice consistently, I believe that you will achieve and maintain greater self-empowerment than ever before.

Where do we go from here? Before storing this book in your library, please read and take to heart my closing comments in the last chapter.

Chapter 19

Where Do We Go from Here?

I can best answer that question by writing what I say to clients: *These techniques only work when you choose to use them.*

For example, when someone pushes one of my buttons and I forget to use my peaceful-place trigger, I get just as stressed as anyone else. I've also endured painful setbacks and have sought hypnotherapy from one of my peers to help me get back on track. At such times, motivation might have been almost impossible without utilizing what I teach. It seems as though an unseen hand often forces me to walk my talk, so that I can more effectively teach these powerful techniques. The empowerment exercises are a blessing to anyone who masters them, so I want to teach them to anyone willing to learn and apply them.

Some of you may also wish to help others.

Helping Friends and Loved Ones

Human nature has some good qualities. We often like to help friends and loved ones by sharing valuable ideas; I sincerely hope you have learned something worthy of sharing with your friends and loved ones. While I hope that you will encourage others to buy this book, I must ask that you think carefully before giving advice to those who need help. Let me speak from my heart.

Over the years, many of my clients have suffered the *added burden of unnecessary guilt*, often compounded by negative criticism from friends, relatives, or loved ones. Criticism from others frequently contributes to a client's difficulty in overcoming a problem. Some put-downs reported to me by clients and friends are:

1. Don't you know smoking will kill you?
2. Fat people are out of control.
3. You have a poverty consciousness.
4. Get out of the victim trap.
5. Why did you create this problem?
6. Why did you make yourself sick?
7. What is God punishing you for?
8. You must have a karmic lesson to learn.

Remarks like these, even if spoken with good intentions, often cause further damage to a person's self-esteem. Such negative criticism disempowers the recipient, often inhibiting his/her ability to overcome negative subconscious programming regardless of whether such negativity was self-created or planted by other people.

Furthermore, when the problem is serious these remarks hurt even more and can tarnish a friendship. If you must say something negative, criticize the performance but not the person.

A friend of mine received hurtful put-downs while trying to escape from an abusive relationship. Prior to marriage, she had no clue whatsoever that the man she loved would become an abusive controller who manipulated with guilt and threats. She needed professional help, not more criticism and guilt; instead, her life was shattered. Unfortunately, the first two counselors she saw asked her what she had done to attract an abuser into her life in the first place! The added stress of that unexpected criticism made her physically ill.

Another friend of mine, who was devoted to a spiritual path, got cancer and lost several alleged friends because she lost her health! She was at peace before her passing, so let anyone who would dare judge her for having a "disease consciousness" consider their own possible reactions in her circumstances.

When you are down, you quickly discover who your true friends are. One of the most profound demonstrations of this fact occurred to me in 1981, after the stress of divorce hurt my ability to sell. I prayed for money just to buy food. The very next day a close friend took me to lunch, handed me a $100 bill, and said: *God directed me to give you my tithe, because you deserve it!* He told me that he derived greater satisfaction giving to people *personally*, rather than through a church or charity just to get the tax deduction. Shortly before that experience, a millionaire who pretended to be my friend had criticized me when I asked for help finding a decent-paying job. I understand the difference between being helped and being kicked when I'm down. It should be obvious which action helped me the most!

If you are blessed with the ability to help a friend-in-need, respond with compassion and generosity, or simply say no kindly. Your friend (or relative) may not yet understand the role of the subconscious. He/she may have suffered financial setbacks resulting from the greed of others. He/she may still live in slavery to past subconscious programming, or have developed illness after repeated setbacks in life. The "tough love" approach just might be the final blow that crushes the person's spirit. While a harsh approach *might* be necessary for someone who is unwilling to change, a gentle approach is far better for someone who has already made a commitment to change.

Even when people successfully change their subconscious programming, they might just need a little outside help to change external circumstances. The motivation may be present, but an obstacle can still look quite large if you have to lift it by yourself. Do we move a heavy piece of furniture alone, or do we get someone to help us lift it? Make a few phone calls. Lend a helping hand. Exchange services if possible and help each other. Hire him/her to do a job for you. Give a gift or loan if you are blessed and so inclined. Be supportive, or just say no. If you are unable or unwilling to help, refer your friend to someone who can do so. Admit that you are too busy if that's the case. You can offer to pray, but don't say anything such as: *I'm being hard on you because I care about you.* I won't put into print what that sounds like to the person who is down!

Instead of criticizing the person, analyze the performance and *offer solutions.* Help empower him or her to obtain the desired results. Share what you've learned from this book (consider giving him/her a copy if you wish). Additionally, encourage your friend to *seek professional and/or spiritual help when appropriate.*

Conclusion

Self-hypnosis helps us make desired changes at a subconscious level, but it should be clear by now that hypnosis is not a panacea for all of life's problems. Wise King Solomon said that there is a time and season for all things. There is a time and a place for self-hypnosis. There are times and places for traditional therapy and for hypnotherapy. Yet even when seeking professional help, *proper use of self-hypnosis* can still provide many benefits to enhance the journey to greater empowerment. (It is also my opinion that both self-hypnosis and hypnotherapy can provide valuable keys to greater spiritual awareness, but that's another book.)

I am totally convinced that trance has a valid place in the world today for all who desire to improve themselves, whether personally, professionally, or spiritually. In my opinion, *trance is the key to helping us attain our ideal self-empowerment.*

We must train ourselves to imagine good things. Lots of people believe in positive thinking yet indulge in negative daydreaming—and wonder why they get negative results. Remember: *it's not what we think; it's what we imagine that usually influences our behavior*—like those who tell themselves not to eat candy while they imagine how good it would taste. Always remember what imagination can do to the subconscious. *Imagination can make or break your success in goal achievement!*

In closing, let me repeat that you *cannot force* your subconscious to accept anything, any more than a high-pressure salesman can force you to buy; that's why willpower has such a low record of success. You must allow your subconscious mind to be *persuaded* to accept the desired changes by getting involved in the benefits.

Additionally, I believe we must learn how to make our subconscious become our servant rather than our slave master. Claim your God-given power of choice. Be the *captain* of your subconscious programming and send your mind-ship at warp speed toward your dreams. Now you have the tools; the rest is up to you. The journey continues... You may now master the power of self-hypnosis to make your best dreams in life come true. Now go, and *make it so!*

THANK YOU for reading *Mastering the Power of Self-hypnosis.* The author sincerely hopes that this book helps you make beneficial changes in your life!

Questions and Answers About Self-Hypnosis

NOTE: I have divided the Appendix into several sections for easy reference. Note that the questions in this section appear in bold print, making it easy to find those questions that interest you. Additionally, note that the questions in this section refer primarily to self-hypnosis rather than hypnosis. If you wish to read the answers to commonly asked questions regarding hypnosis, find a way to get access to the internet. The official FAQ (Frequently Asked Questions) for the worldwide Internet alt.hypnosis newsgroup is stored on my website at: http://www.hunter.holowww.com/HYPNOFAQ.html

Q. What technique is the best?

A. Each of us is *unique* in the universe! I often tell clients, "God didn't make a bunch of yellow pencils." This metaphor serves to illustrate the fact that *no one technique* will work for all the people all the time; so this book presents a variety of techniques to serve the reader. I recommend that you attempt each basic technique at least once (except for techniques designed for specific goals that may be unimportant to you, such as those described in Chapter 14). If you reflect back on my book as a complete presentation, consider that I have given you a foundation to construct your own specific *HypnoCise* program for empowerment. Within that foundation, you may choose your own preferred induction, a unique set of benefits ideally suited to your desires, specific affirmations more suitable to you than to anyone else, and a key word to trigger your new subconscious program. Your personal *HypnoCise* program should be *uniquely suited to you!*

Q. What is the best time of day for self-hypnosis?

A. This varies from person to person. I personally prefer the afternoon. Some people obtain maximum benefit in the early morning, while others find an evening time better. Experiment with various times until you determine your best time.

Q. Should I turn out the lights when I do self-hypnosis?

A. The answer to this question depends on your personal preference. Some people quickly become distracted by light—particularly bright light, which can sometimes penetrate closed eyelids. Some people prefer total darkness. I personally prefer soft lighting. Again, experiment as you wish until you determine what works best for you.

Q. What about background music?

A. Decide according to your desires. Some clients, including many who visualize quite well, prefer total silence. Others enjoy background music. My preference is to use background music whenever possible, as I prefer to focus on the music rather than on other distracting sounds such as traffic, barking dogs, etc. I can also meditate quite easily out in nature with only the natural sounds of nature instead of music. Those of you who love the sounds of nature might find certain nature tapes helpful. Again, experiment until you discover what works best for you.

Q. How did you get interested in hypnosis?

A. When I worked as a highly stressed-out sales manager for a major corporation, I went to a hypnotherapist for stress management. I learned the peaceful-place meditation and a simple stress-coping technique, and my life forever changed. The coping technique has prevented me from buying into stress levels that could have jeopardized my health and possibly even my life; and the peaceful-place meditation (or mental mini-vacation) keeps me calm and centered.

The benefits gained personally from my sessions *as well as learning self-hypnosis* made me appreciate the value of hypnosis. Through the encouragement of friends and family, I studied at the Tebbetts Hypnotism Training Institute in Washington and started full-time hypnotherapy in 1983. Now I *teach* a hypnosis course at a college. My course is based on the teachings of the late Charles Tebbetts.

Q. Can you quit smoking in one session?

A. In this fast food society, people want everything NOW, and yesterday isn't soon enough! Many people have been disillusioned with hypnosis after failing in the quick-fix programs that appeal to those who want something quick and cheap. Although these quickie programs may work for someone who simply needs one extra push to get over the hump, those people who do succeed may put on thirty pounds of weight as a substitute for the discarded fair-weather friend.

If you want to become a tolerant nonsmoker, go to someone who requires three or four visits minimum. Most of my clients do manage to quit smoking at the first session; but a second session devoted to teaching self-hypnosis for stress management increases the long-term probability of success. I include a third session for confidence building and/or to help with trouble spots, as I believe in a much more professional approach. The one-session quick-fix plans fail frequently. (With many smokers, I complete a motivation map involving the five subconscious motivators presented in Chapter 6.)

If you consider attending any of the hotel seminars, remember that you get what you pay for! If you smoked for twenty-nine years, you cannot expect to feel like a nonsmoker in twenty-nine minutes. You may indeed stop lighting a match to your money, but you might feel grief for the loss of your "friend" for many years to come. Furthermore, you especially want to avoid those smoking cessation programs that employ gross aversion techniques. The use of fear motivation pushes the "rebel" button in many people, causing a high backslide rate even with those programs that misrepresent their success rates at 97%. If the success rate sounds too good to be true, it probably is!

Q. Why wasn't self-hypnosis taught during the 1800s?

A. I can only provide a speculative answer to this question: human nature. One who masters self-hypnosis gains greater self-empowerment. Some people derive a certain sort of ego satisfaction by subjugating another person; and it seems that only a very few inside the medical community back then wanted to help *empower* the people to help themselves. Considering the fact that our early researchers of hypnosis believed that the hypnotist had power over the subject, perhaps you might arrive at the same conclusion I have. My opposition to the old "mind control" philosophy is why I object to use of the word *subject* to describe those experiencing hypnosis. That being said, I must also admit that some of our early researchers sincerely *did not know* that any of us could learn how to enter trance without help.

Q. Does hypnosis open your mind up to demonic influence?

A. Some religions frequently make this claim in order to discourage their membership from using hypnosis. If entering the alpha state opens up the mind to demonic influence, then we'd better avoid the following: movies, TV, speeches or sermons at church that cause us to use the imagination, daydreaming, going to sleep, etc. Well, I guess that means we can't tell our children bedtime stories anymore, as their little imaginations run free! Pardon the sarcasm here, but I needed to illustrate my point. Hypnosis of and by itself is neither good nor bad; rather, the specific application of hypnosis (and motives of the hypnotist) will determine whether we can justify its use in any particular situation. Let's use our own intelligence to consider the facts; hopefully we can insure that trance emerges totally out of the Dark Ages once and for all. In my opinion, we must shine the light of truth on hypnosis so that it remains in a state of enlightenment.

Q. Can you share some success stories?

A. Although I can share many success stories, I'll choose one example for each of several common goals...

A smoker taking my hypnotherapy course decided to use self-hypnosis alone to quit, incorporating the benefits approach ("Selling Success to the Subconscious") along with affirmations and key words. He quit totally, and was still a nonsmoker when I last spoke with him (two years after he quit).

I recently met a slender middle-aged woman who claimed that she attended a self-hypnosis class *over ten years ago* taught by Pat Collins in southern California. Before taking that class, she weighed over two hundred pounds. Through self-hypnosis learned in class, she took off over seventy pounds! Furthermore, she expects to remain slender for the rest of her life, and doesn't even think about the fact that she used to be heavy. This woman's success is *profound!* While many of my own clients have successfully reduced, people needing to reduce more than thirty to forty pounds frequently need private sessions as well as self-hypnosis.

A salesman saw me for stress management after being referred by his personal physician. Although I also worked with him for self-confidence, I taught him the stress-coping technique presented in Chapter 8. Mastering self-hypnosis to reduce stress resulted in a significant improvement in his health. Several years later I ran into him at a trade show, and he still used my techniques regularly.

A business owner saw me for professional confidence. I taught him the techniques presented in this book, and three months later he wrote me an excellent letter. Within the first month after completing my program, he closed more business transactions than he normally closed in six months.

A military officer needed to keep calm before taking an exam. Previous failures resulted in his having only one final opportunity to pass, or be retired. He mastered the peaceful-place meditation (mental mini-vacation) and the stress-coping technique. Additionally, he practiced *HypnoCise*. He passed the test and got his promotion!

A black belt in the martial arts mastered self-hypnosis and used the peak-performance trigger, along with "focus" as his key word. He blended frequent visualization along with his sports trigger. He placed in a regional competition.

A realtor increased his income from $28,000 to $130,000 in only one year.

Will self-hypnosis work for you? Master the art and find out for yourself!

Q. If I learn self-hypnosis, when and why would I ever need a hypnotherapist?

A. Refer to the last section of Chapter 14 for that answer.

Q. Is there any danger in learning self-hypnosis?

A. In almost fifteen years of practice, not one of my clients has ever reported any harm resulting from learning self-hypnosis; yet I cannot guarantee that any skill has no potential drawbacks. Driving can be dangerous, but we choose to drive because of the benefits of getting where we need to go. Self-hypnosis can help us get where we need to go mentally. Just as driving is faster than walking, self-hypnosis is faster than willpower.

I believe in balance (or moderation) in all things. Naturally, if someone spent most of the waking hours in a trance, life would simply pass on by with few accomplishments. Also, it would be very unadvisable to attempt self-hypnosis while driving or while operating any type of machinery. Again, *there is a time and place for all things*.

Q. What if self-hypnosis doesn't work?

A. Some people can enter a light state of trance and be unaware of the fact that they have achieved that state. During light states, our sensory perception increases. We have an *increasing* ability to perceive sounds, feelings, etc., and this often distracts the conscious mind. We can easily convince ourselves that something isn't working by using our awareness of the distraction as "proof" that we are still awake! (The mind can think many times faster than the spoken voice.)

Remember that *imagination* is the *language of the subconscious*. Go into your fantasized peaceful place. Try several different inductions if you don't respond to the first one. If necessary, go see a hypnotherapist. Since I could not find a good set of instructions, I experienced great difficulty learning self-hypnosis at first. Finally, a hypnotherapist guided me into a trance and gave me posthypnotic suggestions to enable me to take myself into a trance. Hopefully this book will help you avoid the difficulty I experienced; but if you need help, seek it. For me, the help was worth the price.

Q. How can I choose a qualified hypnotherapist?

A. I must provide a lengthy answer for this question.

Most competent hypnotherapists have completed formal training in hypnotherapy, such as the courses of 150 hours recommended by several professional hypnosis associations. Hypnotherapy is an *art or skill* best learned from those who actually have done considerable hypnotherapy. Ask where your prospective therapist received training, how many hours of schooling he/she took specifically for hypnosis, and whether or not the therapist works full-time with hypnosis. (One who works full-time in hypnotherapy is more likely to have mastered the art than someone who only practices occasionally, although some excellent hypnotherapists do have to work a second just to pay all the bills.) Some people may wish to ask about his/her experience; but realize that *all of us started new at one time,* so please do not disqualify someone simply because he/she is new to the profession.

Additionally, any ethical hypnotherapist should belong to at least one professional hypnosis association, such as the International Medical Dental Hypnotherapy Association, the National Guild of Hypnotists, National Association of Transpersonal Hypnotherapy, the Association to Advance Ethical Hypnosis, and/or a state hypnosis association. If he/she does not belong to at least one professional association that has either the word *hypnosis* or *hypnotherapy* in its name, consider it a yellow light and proceed with caution!

If you choose a physician or Ph.D., you still have the right to ask specifically where he or she received SPECIFIC training in hypnotherapy. Be aware that someone specifically trained in hypnotherapy may quite possibly be far more competent with hypnosis for motivation than a physician (or Ph.D.) who only occasionally practices hypnosis. Having a degree in medicine or psychology does not of and by itself guarantee competency with hypnosis even though there may be competence in the primary field of expertise. Seeking out a physician or psychologist to hypnotize you may result in going to someone who only had a weekend course in hypnosis (or worse, was self-taught). Would you ask your family doctor to work on your teeth?

ANYONE practicing hypnotherapy should, in my opinion, have AT LEAST a minimum of one hundred hours (preferably more) in specialized training in the applications of hypnosis, regardless of other qualifications. In spite of my stated opinion regarding training, however, ethics are more important than training or education. Given the choice, I personally would rather see a new yet ethical hypnotherapist with one hundred hours of training than to go to a well-educated person working from ego or greed.

Sometimes the phone call might leave you in doubt. If your phone discussion does not provide adequate information to make a decision, you may ask your prospective therapist for a short personal consultation to help you decide. Most ethical hypnotherapists are willing to invest twenty to thirty minutes to meet with a prospective client, providing you a free consultation.

Do you still need more information? Log on to the Internet and read the official alt.hypnosis FAQ located on my website (http://www.hunter.holowww.com/HYPNOFAQ.html). Two of those questions pertain to professional hypnosis training, which might help you make a more informed choice.

Q. Do you give presentations or workshops on self-hypnosis?

A. I'm very happy to teach these important techniques to a live audience. Self-hypnosis helped me conquer my own fear of speaking in public, so it's *personal!* Several major hypnosis associations regularly invite me to present workshops at their annual conventions; but it also gives me great satisfaction sharing with people who are new to the wonders of hypnosis.

My topics include those that I presented in this book, as well as professional hypnosis training were appropriate. As time permits, I'm also available for media appearances.

In recent years I've enjoyed presenting for both associations and corporations. If you are interested in hearing me make a presentation, ask your meeting planner or human resource director to contact me for more details. I'm also available for public seminars, provided a local sponsor makes the appropriate arrangements. If interested, contact me at 1-253-927-8888 (serious inquiries only). You may also e-mail me (rhunter@halcyon.com) or write me at:

Roy Hunter
Alliance Hypnotherapy Inc.
30640 Pacific Hwy. S. #E
Federal Way, WA 98003 (USA)

Glossary of Common Hypnosis Terms and Abbreviations

abreaction: emotional discharge, usually due to remembering past pain

affirmations: positive statements designed to change subconscious programming

age regression: guiding a hypnotized person backward in time by his/her age (WARNING: Only those trained in regression therapy should do this!)

alpha: a state of the mind where brainwave activity slows down to a range of from 7 to 14 cycles per second, during which we experience hypnosis, and which we pass through on the way to and from sleep daily

altered consciousness: synonymous with alpha; terminology used to refer to the state of mind we experience during hypnosis, meditation, or any form of trance

anchoring: establishing a trigger that, when activated, will trigger certain responses; this happens randomly in life, but can be suggested during hypnosis (*see also* triggers)

aversion suggestion: suggestions given that emphasize negative aspects of a habit, such as finding smoke to smell horrible and/or make someone sick

awakening: the act of bringing a person up out of trance and into full conscious awareness

beta: that state of mind we are in during most of our waking hours, the thinking mode

deepening: in hypnosis, this refers to attaining a more profound trance state

delta: that state of mind we enter during deep sleep, total unconsciousness

direct suggestion: suggestion given as a command ("take a deep breath")

expectancy: having expectations of a certain outcome

eye-fixation: induction involving staring at an object

false memories: fantasies that are experienced during a mishandled regression and are believed to be repressed memories rather than fantasies

FMS: abbreviation for False Memory Syndrome (having false memories)

Gestalt therapy: involves role-playing (often used for release)

HypnoCise: a word coined by the FAQ author to describe the combination of imagery, meditation, self-hypnosis, and properly constructed affirmations

hypnosis: a trance state that is guided by someone or something other than the person experiencing the trance (there are numerous definitions by different experts)

hypnotherapist: a trained professional who uses hypnosis to help people with self-improvement and/or for therapeutic purposes

hypnotherapy: the use of hypnosis for self-improvement and/or for therapeutic purposes

hypnotist: anyone who guides another person into hypnosis

ideomotor responding: having client answer questions via finger movement

imagery: using the imagination to fantasize or remember events

indirect suggestion: permissive suggestion ("you can take a deep breath whenever you wish to relax")

induction: a technique that guides (induces) a person into a hypnotic state

initial sensitizing event: an emotional event that is the ORIGIN of a problem, creating a sensitivity to feelings, such as tracing claustrophobia back to being locked in a closet at age three

ISE: abbreviation for Initial Sensitizing Event

NLP: abbreviation for Neuro-Linguistic Programming, a modality of change that evolved from the teachings of Milton Erickson

NS: abbreviation for Non-Smoking programs

old tapes: a term frequently used to describe memories that are replayed in the imagination in a manner that may influence our behavior and/or attitudes

original sensitizing event: alternate name for initial sensitizing event

parts therapy: a complex hypnotic technique where the therapist talks with various parts of the mind, such as the inner child and inner adult (WARNING: Only those trained in parts therapy should use it!)

past-life therapy: regression into real or imagined past life

PLR: abbreviation for Past-Life Regression

PLT: abbreviation for Past-Life Therapy (PLR is used more often)

posthypnotic suggestion: a suggestion given during the trance state that is acted upon after emerging from the trance state

PR: abbreviation for Progressive Relaxation

progressive relaxation: a type of induction involving the progressive relaxation of various parts of the body

PT: abbreviation for Parts Therapy

rapport: a comfortable feeling between client and hypnotist resulting in a level of trust and a greater ability to respond to suggestion

reframing: using the imagination to imagine a different outcome of a past event, such as combining Gestalt therapy with regression therapy to facilitate release; also used in NLP with guided imagery

regression: going back in time during trance to remember past events, and replaying them in the imagination, often with accompanying emotions

self-hypnosis: a self-induced trance state

stage hypnosis: the public use of hypnosis purely for entertainment purposes

subconscious: that part of our mind that is the seat of imagination, emotion, artistic abilities, and other skills, and takes care of numerous functions without our conscious awareness, such as automatic functions of our organs, etc.

subjects (of hypnosis): the term used by many to describe a person who is in hypnosis (NOTE: the word *client* is used with increasing frequency by hypnotherapists)

systematic desensitization: the use of programmed imagery in a systematic way to help desensitize someone from an anxiety or phobia

theta: that state of the mind we are in while dreaming

time distortion: the term for a unique phenomenon where we lose conscious awareness of how much time has passed (examples: five minutes can seem like twenty minutes, or vice versa)

trigger: something seen, heard, felt, etc., that "triggers" a response, urge, memory, or emotion, etc., such as turning the key in the car might trigger a smoker to light up a cigarette

WT: abbreviation for WeighT

zzz: sleeeeeeeeep (go waaaaay down deep!)

NOTE: This glossary appears in the official alt.hypnosis FAQ on the Internet.

Affirmations and Scripts

Instructions

The affirmations in this section provide a foundation for constructing your own personalized affirmations for *HypnoCise*. You may use these as you wish, modifying them and/or adding additional ones in accordance with the guidelines provided in Chapters 15 and 16.

If you wish to make a cassette tape, change the affirmations from the first-person to the second person ("I am" becomes "You are," etc.). Additionally, note the inclusion of full scripts (in the second-person format) for weight management, smoking cessation, and smoking reduction. Should you wish to utilize one of these three scripts, either have someone read the script to you, or record the script in its entirety for playback. Note that the scripts are designed for the *subconscious* and do not follow strict rules of grammar.

Affirmations for Confidence

1. Each day I go through my daily activities with a confident and controlled attitude.
2. I am calm, relaxed, and confident.
3. My new self-image makes it easier to go through all my daily activities with increasing confidence and success.
4. I enjoy peace, health, and greater happiness in all my endeavors.
5. Whenever I desire extra confidence, I simply take a deep breath and feel more calm and confident as I exhale.
6. I am grateful for all that contributes daily to my increasing confidence.
7. I am an expert in my profession.
8. I handle all areas of my chosen profession easily and confidently.
9. The many and varied situations in which I find myself are always handled competently in a calm, relaxed manner.
10. I do all things well. I look my best in all situations, and work my best.
11. My conversation is natural and easy, and my confident attitude attracts success.
12. I always act, feel, and think as my new self-image.
13. My confidence increases daily.
14. I am now and ever shall remain as my new self-image.
15. I love myself now.
16. I claim and attain empowerment, and I now allow my desire to become my reality.

Affirmations for Learning and Study Habits

1. I am calm, relaxed, and confident about my personal learning processes. I accomplish more in shorter periods of time and my work shows an increasing accuracy and understanding. This is my self-image.

2. Whenever I read or hear material I wish to know and remember, I find my memory is crystal clear. I easily recall whatever is desired or required. My mind is always calm, relaxed, efficient, and orderly.
3. When I study I have increasing ability to concentrate for longer periods of time as I choose, excluding all common distractions. My comprehension and recall improve daily.
4. I easily present whatever is desired or required—whether orally, in written form, or by demonstration. I always communicate easily and effortlessly.
5. My memory improves daily. My habits and attitudes reflect my confident self-image.
6. Every day in every way I find it easier to study, recall, and present information and remain in total self-control. I am now and ever shall remain as my new self-image.
7. I claim and attain empowerment, and I now allow my desire to become my reality.

Affirmations for Stress Management

1. I am calm, relaxed, and self-confident. I think of myself this way. It is easy to be efficient and effective and still be calm and composed.
2. Each time I retire, I fall into a deep, restful, and peaceful sleep. I awaken at my desired time happy, refreshed, and ready for new activity.
3. When I wish to sleep, I take several deep breaths and think the words *relax and sleep* and easily drift into a deep slumber.
4. Whenever something happens that used to push my buttons, I simply take a deep breath and remain calm. While exhaling, I think the word *relax* and am free to think with a clear mind and use my best wisdom, knowledge, understanding, training, and experience to make the best decision.
5. I like myself now, and I am in control of my emotions.
6. Every day in every way I am more relaxed, calm, and composed. I am now and ever shall remain as my new self-image.
7. I claim and attain empowerment, and I now allow my desire to become my reality.

Affirmations for Success

1. I am increasingly poised and successful in all situations. I know that my successful self-image improves and matures each day.
2. Every day I am influenced by whatever benefits me and my objectives. My activities add to my health, my strength, my energy, my prosperity, and my peace of mind, and every day in every way I get closer and closer to my ideal image.
3. I am happy and healthy.
4. My conversation is natural and easy, and my confident attitude attracts success. I use my talents wisely and efficiently.
5. I have my life plan well defined and organized, and my priorities and goals are clear.
6. I work efficiently with determination to bring my desires into reality because I control my own destiny. I excel at what I do, and I remember to recognize and celebrate my successes.
7. My relations with people continually become more pleasing and effective. I talk to people easily and naturally on first acquaintance and I initiate the conversation. I expect to do this. Any time I take a deep breath and think of this expectation, it gains strength and permanence.
8. What others might call problems are simply opportunities for growth. I know that the best answers present themselves in deep states of relaxation.

9. Through the power of love, I am abundantly successful. I am worthy of my success, and I accept my success naturally and gratefully. I am and ever shall remain as my new self-image.
10. I claim and attain empowerment, and I now allow my desire to become my reality.

Affirmations for Weight Management

1. I like myself and believe in myself.
2. I desire to be at my healthiest, most ideal weight because I am worth it.
3. I enjoy eating the right amounts of those foods that help me reach and maintain my healthiest, ideal body weight. By eating slowly, I am satisfied with appropriate amounts of the right foods and am pleasantly satisfied from meal to meal.
4. Every day in every way I find it easier to be totally self-motivated to do what is wise to help me reach and maintain my healthiest, ideal body weight.
5. I make wise choices about my health and eating habits.
6. I am totally satisfied with the wise choices I make regarding the foods I eat.
7. Every time I choose water or a noncaloric beverage in-between meals, my choice satisfies me, because I love my power of choice. And like a muscle that's used is stronger with use, my power of choice is stronger with use—so every wise choice increases my motivation and confidence.
8. With each passing day, my new slim, trim image becomes more and more real. I always think, act, and move as this new self-image. As my new image becomes more and more real in my mind, it becomes more and more real in my body.
9. I claim and attain empowerment, and I now allow my desire to become my reality.

Weight-management Script

Read the italicized print into the tape recorder (or to the person entering self-hypnosis). The words in normal print are instructions for the person reading the script. Emphasize the words in CAPS, saying them slowly and with feeling. Pause briefly wherever you see three dots (...). Review the script at least once before using it to become familiar with its content and the instructions. Have your list of benefits and affirmations handy.

Begin with the progressive relaxation induction from Chapter 4, then continue...

Now imagine you are already at your ideal, healthiest body weight. You LOVE how you look and feel. Imagine standing in front of a mirror, seeing a reflection of yourself wearing the size clothes you choose to wear. These clothes LOOK good, and they FEEL good, and they fit well on you. Now imagine doing something you totally enjoy doing at your ideal weight. Just BE there in your mind... and ENJOY.

(Extra pause...)

Imagine your personal benefits...

(Take list of personal benefits and read them one by one, SLOWLY...)

Now imagine your MOST IMPORTANT BENEFITS SO VIVIDLY that you feel as though you already enjoy success... Imagine your benefits... SO VIVIDLY... that you FEEL as though you already... ENJOY... SUCCESS!

(Extra pause...)

The terms are so simple. You simply use your power of choice to CHOOSE what goes into your mouth... when, where, and how much. YOU decide what goes into your mouth... when, where, and how much... and you have an increasing satisfaction from the right amounts of those foods that help you reach your ideal, healthiest body weight... And you make wise choices about your health and eating habits. Also, whenever you choose water or a noncaloric beverage to satisfy an in between meal snack urge, you are TOTALLY satisfied, physically, mentally, and emotionally, because YOU CHOSE...

You LOVE your power of choice. And like a muscle that's used becomes stronger with use, your power of choice becomes stronger with use. Imagine using that power of choice right now to choose water or a noncaloric beverage. And when you've successfully practiced this imagery in your mind, either move a finger or take one deep breath...

(Extra pause...)

Very good. Like a muscle that's used becomes stronger with use, your power of choice becomes stronger with use... and every time you make a wise choice, it becomes even easier to make wise choices, because the BENEFITS are so satisfying, and you LOVE your power of choice!

(NOTE: If you eat too fast, SLOWLY read next paragraph... otherwise, skip it.)

Also, whenever you eat, you eat SLOWLY... enough to ENJOY... the FLAVOR of EACH BITE... And when you have had enough food to give your body nourishment, you feel satisfied, physically, mentally, and emotionally. And every day it becomes easier for you to be TOTALLY self-motivated to do those things that help you reach your ideal body weight, because you love the benefits.

Now imagine you are already at your ideal, healthiest body weight. You LOVE how you look and feel... Imagine standing in front of a mirror seeing a reflection of yourself wearing the size clothes you choose to wear. These clothes LOOK good, and they FEEL good, and they fit well on you. Now imagine doing something you totally enjoy doing at your ideal weight. Just BE THERE in your mind... and ENJOY.

(Read affirmations slowly, in the second-person.)

* * * [affirmations] * * *

(Extra pause. Say the next paragraph SLOWLY...)

Now imagine your MOST IMPORTANT BENEFITS SO VIVIDLY that you feel as though you already enjoy success... Imagine your benefits SO VIVIDLY... that you FEEL... as though you already ENJOY... SUCCESS!

You have chosen the benefits because you absolutely deserve them. KNOW that you deserve the benefits. You LOVE your power of choice and every day it becomes easier and easier for you to be TOTALLY self-motivated to make wise choices about your health and your eating habits... And like a muscle that's used becomes stronger with use, your power of choice becomes stronger with use... giving you a GREATER STRENGTH OF WILL THAN YOU HAVE EVER KNOWN BEFORE...

(Extra pause...)

And now, as I give you some silence, once again imagine your success SO VIVIDLY that all of these affirmations simply go deeper and deeper into your subconscious, becoming a part of you simply because you choose them.

(Extra pause...)

Now, I am going to count from one up to five and then I am going to say "fully aware." At the count of five, let your eyelids open and you are calm, refreshed, relaxed, fully aware, and normal in every way.

One... Slowly, calmly, easily, and gently you are returning to your full awareness once again.

Two... Each muscle and nerve in your body is loose, limp, and relaxed, and you feel wonderfully good.

Three... From head to toe you are feeling perfect in every way... physically perfect, mentally alert, and emotionally serene... and when you get behind the wheel of your vehicle, you are totally alert in every way, responding appropriately to any and all traffic situations.

Number four... Your eyes begin to feel sparkling clear, just as though they were bathed in fresh spring water. On the next number now, let your eyelids open and you are then calm, rested, refreshed, fully aware, and feeling good in every way.

Number five... Eyelids open now. You are fully aware once again. Take a deep breath, fill up your lungs, and stretch.

Smoking-cessation Script

Read the italicized print into the tape recorder (or to the person entering self-hypnosis). The words in normal print are instructions for the person reading the script. Emphasize the words in CAPS, saying them slowly and with feeling. Pause briefly wherever you see three dots (...). Review the script at least once before using it to become familiar with its content and the instructions. Have your list of benefits handy, plus any personal affirmations should you choose to add them.

Begin with the progressive relaxation induction from Chapter 4, then continue...

Your imagination is the rehearsal room of your mind... and you have TOTAL POWER and TOTAL FREEDOM to DO anything you wish and to BE anywhere you wish. In your mind, you can move through time and space...

Now imagine this is one year from today, and you have already been a totally tolerant nonsmoker for one year. Your lungs reward you for the fresh air you give them and you LOVE how you feel... physically, mentally, and emotionally.

(Extra pause...)

Imagine your personal benefits...

(Take list of personal benefits and read them one by one, SLOWLY...)

Now imagine your MOST IMPORTANT BENEFIT SO VIVIDLY that you feel as though you already enjoy success.

(Read next paragraph slowly...)

Imagine your benefits... SO VIVIDLY... that you feel as though you already enjoy SUCCESS! If you choose these benefits for yourself, then indicate that choice to yourself right now by moving one of your index fingers or by taking one deep breath...

(Extra pause...)

You have used your power of choice to choose your benefits. The terms are so simple... you simply use that same power of choice to choose ONE DEEP BREATH any time an old light-up trigger occurs, allowing ONE DEEP BREATH to become a TOTALLY SATISFYING REPLACEMENT for yesterday's fair-weather friend. The physical replacement for yesterday's breath of smoke is one deep breath of air. The mental replacement for yesterday's urge is your new friend, FREEDOM to focus your mind or imagination on whatever you choose, because you love your power of choice...

You LOVE your power of choice... and like a muscle that's used becomes stronger with use, your power of choice becomes stronger with use. Imagine using that power of choice right now by imagining a situation that used to trigger a light-up. Now take a deep breath and RELAX... CHOOSE something fun, enjoyable, beautiful, or pleasant to imagine. Indicate to yourself that you have successfully done that by moving a finger or taking one deep breath.

(Extra pause...)

Very good. Like a muscle that's used becomes stronger with use, your power of choice becomes stronger with use... and every time you take that one deep breath, it becomes easier and easier to choose the deep breath instead of the old slave master.

You are a nonsmoker now, because the BENEFITS are so satisfying, and you

LOVE your power of choice! Now once again imagine another old light-up trigger. As you do, take a deep breath and RELAX. Now imagine something fun, enjoyable, beautiful, or pleasant. As you do, you are already practicing your ability to use your new power and friend, FREEDOM, to be a nonsmoker...

Whenever you use your power of choice to focus your mind on whatever you choose, yesterday's urges are simply forgotten... fading away into the mists of time, vanishing into the fog of forgetfulness, replaced with your new friend, FREEDOM... to focus your mind, thoughts, or actions on WHATEVER YOU CHOOSE, whether at work or play, at home or away from home, alone or with others. You have the power of choice. You LOVE your power of choice, and it was YOUR CHOICE to become a nonsmoker... and it is YOUR CHOICE to put your mind or imagination on WHATEVER YOU CHOOSE. And YOUR DECISION is bringing you the benefits you have chosen...

(Include personal affirmations here if desired.)

* * * [affirmations] * * *

(Extra pause... Speak slowly and with feeling.)

Now, once again, imagine your MOST IMPORTANT BENEFITS SO VIVIDLY that you FEEL as though you already ENJOY success... Imagine your benefits... SO VIVIDLY... that you feel as though you already... enjoy SUCCESS!

You have chosen the benefits because you absolutely deserve them. KNOW that you deserve the benefits. You LOVE your power of choice; and every day it becomes easier and easier for you automatically to take that deep breath at times you used to light-up... and as you do, you feel more and more like a nonsmoker with each passing day, as the deep breath becomes a TOTALLY satisfying replacement for yesterday's fair-weather friend.

Your new friend, FREEDOM, becomes so much more satisfying that you simply allow your subconscious to accept that you are now a nonsmoker simply because you chose to be, and you love your power of choice... and every time you say, see, hear, or think the word RELAX, it automatically reinforces all these affirmations. Whenever you say, see, hear, or think the word RELAX, it becomes easier and easier to be totally self-motivated to act like a nonsmoker and remain a nonsmoker, because YOU CHOSE...

(Pause briefly...)

And now, as I give you some silence, once again imagine your success SO VIVIDLY that all of these ideas and suggestions simply go deeper and deeper into your subconscious, becoming a part of you simply because you choose them. And when you again hear my voice, it will be almost time to come back.

(Pause for about thirty seconds...)

Now, I am going to count from one up to five and then I am going to say "fully aware." At the count of five, let your eyelids open and you are calm, refreshed, relaxed, fully aware, and normal in every way.

One... Slowly, calmly, easily, and gently you are returning to your full awareness once again.

Two... Each muscle and nerve in your body is loose, limp, and relaxed, and you feel wonderfully good.

Three... From head to toe you are feeling perfect in every way... physically perfect, mentally alert, and emotionally serene... and when you get behind the wheel of your vehicle, you are totally alert in every way, responding appropriately to any and all traffic situations.

Number four... Your eyes begin to feel sparkling clear, just as though they were bathed in fresh spring water. On the next number now, let your eyelids open and you are then calm, rested, refreshed, fully aware, and feeling good in every way.

Number five... Eyelids open now. You are fully aware once again. Take a deep breath, fill up your lungs, and stretch.

Smoking-reduction Script

Read the italicized print into the tape recorder (or to the person entering self-hypnosis). The words in normal print are instructions for the person reading the script. Emphasize the words in CAPS, saying them slowly and with feeling. Pause briefly wherever you see three dots (...). Review the script at least once before using it, in order to become familiar with both its content and the instructions. Have your list of benefits handy, plus any personal affirmations should you choose to add them. Notice this script contains the word *try*—which implies failure. NEVER use the word *try* unless you do *not* want the subconscious to accept what immediately follows.

Begin with the progressive relaxation induction from Chapter 4, then continue...

Your imagination is the rehearsal room of your mind... and you have TOTAL POWER and TOTAL FREEDOM to DO anything you wish, and to BE anywhere you wish. In your mind, you can move through time and space...

Now imagine yourself as a totally controlled smoker, and you light up ONLY when you consciously choose. Your lungs reward you for the fresh air you give them and you LOVE how you feel... physically, mentally, and emotionally. You find that only a few chosen puffs can give you far more satisfaction than letting the cigarette try to control you.

(Extra pause...)

Imagine your personal benefits...

(Take list of personal benefits and read them one by one, SLOWLY...)

Now imagine your MOST IMPORTANT BENEFIT SO VIVIDLY that you feel as though you already enjoy success.

(Read next paragraph slowly...)

Imagine your benefits... SO VIVIDLY... that you feel as though you already enjoy SUCCESS! If you choose these benefits for yourself, then indicate that choice to yourself right now by moving one of your index fingers or by taking one deep breath...

(Extra pause...)

You have used your power of choice to choose your benefits. The terms are so simple... you simply use that same power of choice to choose ONE DEEP BREATH any time an old light-up trigger occurs, allowing ONE DEEP BREATH to become a TOTALLY SATISFYING REPLACEMENT for yesterday's fair-weather friend. The physical replacement for any automatic light-up is one deep breath of air. You smoke ONLY when you consciously choose, because you love your power of choice... and when you do smoke, you pay total attention to each and every puff, so that a little satisfies more...

You LOVE your power of choice... and like a muscle that's used becomes stronger with use, your power of choice becomes stronger with use. Imagine using that power of choice right now by imagining a situation that used to trigger an automatic light-up. Now take a deep breath and RELAX... CHOOSE something fun, enjoyable, beautiful, or pleasant to imagine. Indicate to yourself that you have successfully done that by moving a finger or taking one deep breath.

(Extra pause...)

Very good. Like a muscle that's used becomes stronger with use, your power of choice becomes stronger with use... and every time you take that one deep breath, it becomes easier and easier to choose the deep breath instead of the old slave master... because YOU have the power of choice. You are MUCH smarter than the cigarette! You have a mind, and you can CHOOSE when or whether to smoke...

You smoke only when you consciously choose... and the BENEFITS are so satisfying... and you LOVE your power of choice! Now once again imagine another old light-up trigger. As you do, take a deep breath and RELAX. Now imagine something fun, enjoy-

able, beautiful or pleasant. As you do, you are already practicing your ability to use your new power and friend, FREEDOM, to CHOOSE...

Whenever you use your power of choice to focus your mind on whatever you choose, yesterday's urges are simply forgotten... fading away into the mists of time, vanishing into the fog of forgetfulness, replaced with your new friend, FREEDOM... to focus your mind, thoughts, or actions on WHATEVER YOU CHOOSE, whether at work or play, at home or away from home, alone or with others. You have the power of choice. You LOVE your power of choice, and it is YOUR CHOICE to tell the cigarette what to do... whether to get lost or get smoked... and it is YOUR CHOICE to put your mind or imagination on WHATEVER YOU CHOOSE. And YOUR DECISION is bringing you the benefits you have chosen...

(Include personal affirmations here if desired.)

*** [affirmations] ***

(Extra pause... Speak slowly and with feeling.)

Now, once again, imagine your MOST IMPORTANT BENEFITS SO VIVIDLY that you FEEL as though you already ENJOY success... Imagine your benefits... SO VIVIDLY... that you feel as though you already... enjoy SUCCESS!

You have chosen the benefits because you absolutely deserve them. KNOW that you deserve the benefits. You LOVE your power of choice; and every day it becomes easier and easier for you automatically to take that deep breath at times you used to light up... and as you do, you feel more and more in control... and the deep breath becomes a TOTALLY satisfying replacement for yesterday's automatic light-ups... Your new friend, FREEDOM, becomes so much more satisfying that you simply allow your subconscious to accept that you smoke only when you consciously choose, and you love your power of choice... and every time you say, see, hear, or think the word RELAX, it automatically reinforces all these affirmations. Whenever you say, see, hear, or think the word RELAX, it becomes easier and easier to be totally self-motivated to be an occasional smoker, because YOU CHOSE... and if and when you ever decide to quit totally, it will be when and if YOU CHOOSE...

(Pause briefly...)

And now, as I give you some silence, once again imagine your success SO VIVIDLY that all of these ideas and suggestions simply go deeper and deeper into your subconscious, becoming a part of you simply because you choose them. And when you again hear my voice, it will be almost time to come back.

(Pause for about thirty seconds...)

Now, I am going to count from one up to five and then I am going to say "fully aware." At the count of five, let your eyelids open and you are calm, refreshed, relaxed, fully aware, and normal in every way.

One... Slowly, calmly, easily, and gently you are returning to your full awareness once again.

Two... Each muscle and nerve in your body is loose, limp, and relaxed, and you feel wonderfully good.

Three... From head to toe you are feeling perfect in every way... physically perfect, mentally alert, and emotionally serene... and when you get behind the wheel of your vehicle, you are totally alert in every way, responding appropriately to any and all traffic situations.

Number four... Your eyes begin to feel sparkling clear, just as though they were bathed in fresh spring water. On the next number now, let your eyelids open and you are then calm, rested, refreshed, fully aware, and feeling good in every way.

Number five... Eyelids open now. You are fully aware once again. Take a deep breath, fill up your lungs, and stretch.

Copyright Warning

My scripts are copyrighted (1993, revised 1997) and are intended only for the personal use of the purchaser of this book. Any unauthorized distribution in any format (including audio-tape) without the written consent of the copyright holder will be considered an infringement of copyright.

Bibliography

Brown, Barbara, *Stress and the Art of Biofeedback*. New York: Bantam Books, 1978.

Coue, Emile, *Self Mastery Through Conscious Autosuggestion*. Kessinger Publishing Company. Montana: 1922.

Darnton, Robert, *Mesmerism and the End of Enlightenment in France*. Cambridge, Mass.: Harvard University Press, 1968.

Elman, Dave, *Hypnotherapy*. Glendale, Calif.: Westwood Publishing, 1970.

Gawain, Shakti, *Creative Visualization*, San Rafael, Calif.: New World Library, 1990, 23rd printing.

Hill, Napoleon, *Think and Grow Rich*. New York: Hawthorn Books, 1966.

LeCron, Leslie M., and Jean Bordeaux, *Hypnotism Today*. North Hollywood, Calif.: Wilshire Book Co., 1947.

McGill, Ormond, *Hypnotism & Meditation: The Operational Manual for Hypnomeditation*. Glendale, Calif.: Westwood Publishing, 1981.

Parkhill, Stephen C., *Answer Cancer, Answers for Living: The Healing of a Nation*. Deerfield Beach, Fla.: Health Communications, 1995.

Russell, James, *Psychosemantic Parenthetics*, Institute of Hypnotechnology (out of print).

Siegel, Bernie S., *Love, Medicine & Miracles: Lessons Learned about Self-Healing from a Surgeon's Experience with Exceptional Patients*. New York: Harper & Row, 1986.

Spanos, Nicholas, and John Chaves, *Hypnosis: The Cognitive Behavioral Perspective*.

Tebbetts, Charles, *Miracles on Demand*, 2nd edition, Thompson/Shore (out of print).

Tebbetts, Charles, *Self-Hypnosis and Other Mind-Expanding Techniques*. Glendale, Calif.: Westwood Publishing, 1977.

Teitelbaum, Myron, *Hypnosis Induction Technics: with a Foreword by Michael M. Gilbert*. Springfield, Ill.: Charles C. Thomas, 1965.

Zanuso, Billa, *The Young Freud: The Origins of Psychoanalysis in Late Nineteenth-Century Viennese Culture*. Oxford, UK; New York: Blackwell, 1986.

Index

About the Author

Roy Hunter, M.S., C.Ht., is a Hypnotherapist certified by several hypnotherapy associations, and a certified hypnotherapy instructor. Roy began a full-time hypnotherapy practice in 1983 and started teaching professional hypnotherapy at Tacoma Community College in 1987. In early 1998, he was invited to teach hypnosis as an adjunct faculty member of Bastyr University. He was personally trained by the legendary late Charles Tebbetts. Roy has received high praise and national recognition for two hypnosis texts (by another publisher) based on the teachings of his late mentor, and has taught advanced hypnosis workshops on both coasts. He authored the official FAQ for the worldwide alt.hypnosis Internet newsgroup. Roy's national honors include Outstanding Service Award (National Guild of Hypnotists), the IHHF award for having the 1990 Hypnotic Voice of the Year, and the Thomas A. Raffa Memorial Award for outstanding achievements and pursuit of excellence in his profession.